HIDDEN HISTORY *of* ST. PETERSBURG

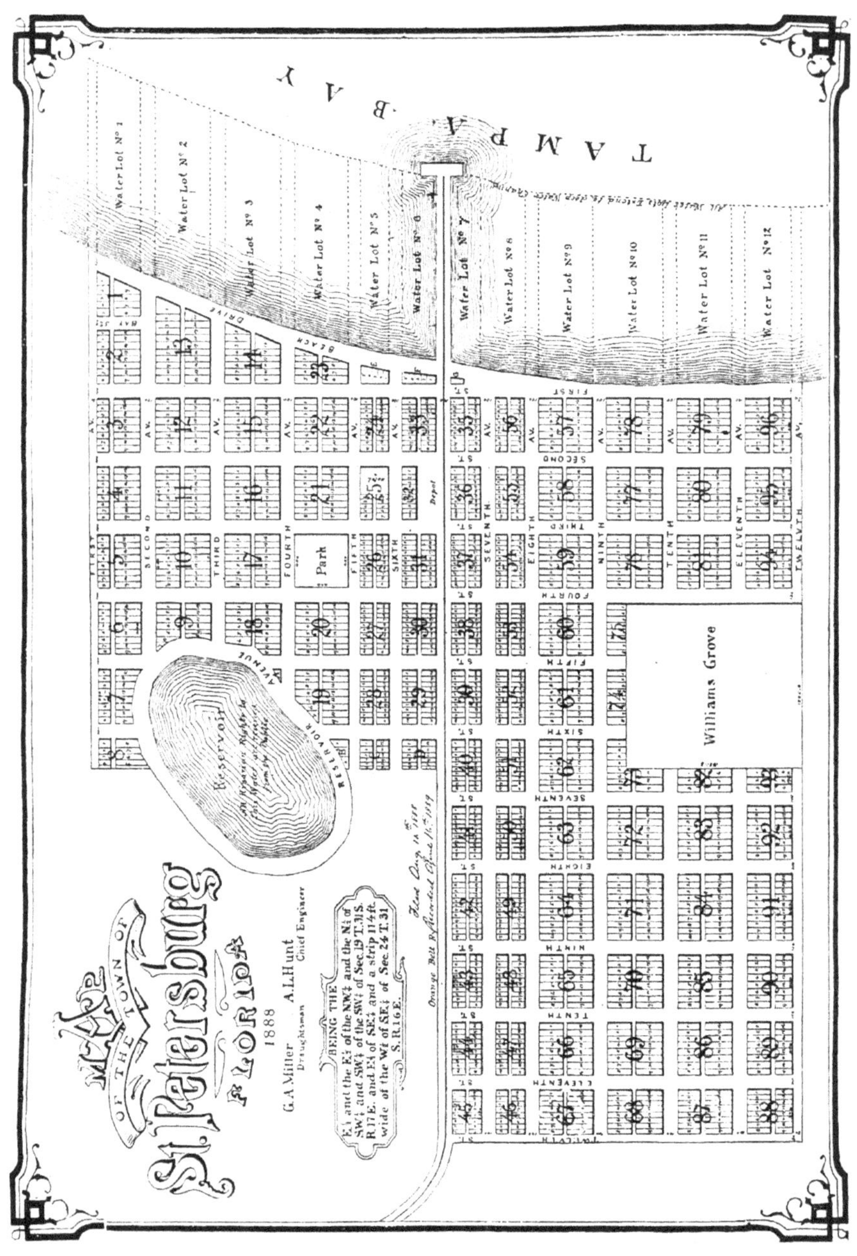

Original town plat for St. Petersburg, dated 1888 and filed by Peter Demens. 6th Avenue later became Central Avenue. Reservoir Lake became Mirror Lake. Williams Park is shown as "Park." *Courtesy St. Petersburg Museum of History.*

HIDDEN HISTORY *of* ST. PETERSBURG

Will Michaels

Foreword *by* Jon Wilson

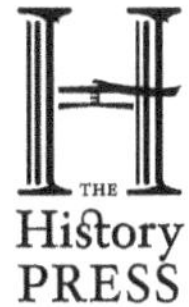

Published by The History Press
Charleston, SC
www.historypress.net

Cover image by Foley & Fisher Real Estate and Fire Insurance, Detroit Publishing Company; courtesy of Michaels Family Collection.

First published 2016

Manufactured in the United States

ISBN 978.1.46713.541.2

Library of Congress Control Number: 2016932071

Dedicated to St. Petersburg's family of historians, including:

John A. Bethell (1914)
Karl H. Grismer (1924)
William L. Straub (1929)
Walter P. Fuller (1973)
Gay Blair White and Warren Brown (1984)
Rita Slaght Gould (1987)
Albert Parry (1987)
Raymond Arsenault (1988)
Thomas Reilly (1997)
Bruce R. Stevenson (1997)
Rick Baker (2000)
Scott Taylor Hartzell (2002)
Sandra W. Rooks (2003)
Gary R. Mormino (2005)
Jon Wilson and Rosalie Peck (2006)
Judy Lowe Wells (2006)
Nevin D. Sitler and Richard N. Sitler (2013)
…and others

Dates denote first published work.

CONTENTS

Foreword

People who love St. Petersburg will love its *Hidden History*. Author Will Michaels, a meticulous historian, offers a journey through a wonderland of Sunshine City stories, familiar but painted with rare affection and detail. For example, many know about early philanthropist Edwin Tomlinson, whose name remains associated with several St. Petersburg landmarks. But who knew that the (arguably) eccentric entrepreneur built a two-hundred-foot wooden tower at his house? And why? Far be it from this foreword to provide spoilers. *Hidden History of St. Petersburg* will tell all.

Mining the lore and legend—and sorting out the useful gems—marks the book's feature characteristic. Al Capone in town back in the Roaring Twenties? This lovely and lively rumor has been around for decades, and Michaels sets us straight. The first shopping center? It was not Central Plaza. In fact, there were two that predate the sprawling mid-twentieth-century retail center. Their locations may surprise you. The storied Manhattan Casino on segregated St. Petersburg's main African American thoroughfare? James Brown, the "Godfather of Soul," played there; Michaels tells the story of the local musician whom Brown "adopted."

A powerful note begins the book. Among St. Petersburg's more secluded secrets are remains of the Tocobaga Indian settlements that thrived here long before 1492, and Michaels points out the tribe's mounds and what they tell us about the ancient native civilization. After the opening chapter, Michaels employs some of each era's luminaries (and characters) to help guide us virtually to the present. Along the way, he sketches the dynamics and the personalities behind the remarkable revival downtown that took place starting in the 1990s and continues now. It is among the first written descriptions of what will certainly be viewed by later historians as a pivotal time in the St. Petersburg story. For political buffs, there is a detailed chapter about St. Petersburg's voting profile in presidential elections from 1952 through 1984. And the rationing, "meatless Tuesdays" and lookouts positioned atop the Vinoy recall the tense times of World War II.

On the lighter side, Michaels takes up the question of Babe Ruth's longest home run and includes a rare and extensive interview he conducted with the Bambino's daughter. He recounts the accomplishments of the society ladies whose Woman's Town Improvement Association brought St. Petersburg many of its early improvements—over the harrumphing of some St. Petersburg men who considered the doughty Victorians to be meddlers. The WTIA, by the way, held its first meeting in the venerable Detroit Hotel, where musical legend Jim Morrison played a gig or two during his early days here.

Local personalities and names somehow familiar do bring *Hidden History of St. Petersburg* a sweet local flavor. Figures such as retail genius James Earl "Doc" Webb and waterfront visionary William L. Straub of course get their due. So does St. Petersburg's history community, either in the text or in the rich notes at the end of each chapter. Readers will recognize such names as Ray Arsenault, Gary Mormino, former mayor Rick Baker and the late Scott Hartzell, along with earlier chroniclers like John Bethell, Karl Grismer and Walter Fuller. Their works are referenced often. Other folks pop up like faces at family reunions. There's Jeff Moshier, who became the *Evening Independent* sports editor right out of high school; Reverend James L. Duncan, missionary rector at St. Peter's Cathedral; aviation historians Warren Brown and Tom Reilly; Dr. Ralph Wimbish, the civil rights activist who died young; dramatist Bill Leavengood and composer Lee Ahlin, who collaborated to produce *Webb's City: The Musical*; Beach Drive developers Jack Bowman and Mike Cheezem; Marty and Elaine Normile, long associated with downtown and the Vinoy Resort; lifelong residents Nancy Osmon Haak and Betsy Pheil; and more and more.

Read every word. You will have embraced St. Petersburg as never before.

—JON WILSON
Florida Humanities Council

Jon Wilson is a lifelong journalist serving as a reporter and editor for the Evening Independent *and* St. Petersburg Times *(now the* Tampa Bay Times*). He is* *co-author with Rosalie Peck of* St. Petersburg's Historic 22nd Street South *and* St. Petersburg's Historic African American Neighborhoods *and author of* The Golden Era in St. Petersburg: Postwar Prosperity in the Sunshine City. *He is also the author of the Cracker Western novel* Bridger's Run. *Jon is currently a communications consultant with the Florida Humanities Council.*

Preface

History does not refer merely to the past. On the contrary, the great force of history comes from the fact that we carry it within us, are unconsciously controlled by it in many ways, and history is literally present in all that we do.
—James S. Baldwin

Like my first book, *The Making of St. Petersburg*, this work is a selection of articles originally published by the St. Petersburg *Northeast Journal*. The articles have been updated to reflect more recent information. The *Journal* is a small but worthy publication primarily distributed in the northeast area of St. Petersburg. I have been writing a history column for the *Journal* for over ten years now. My first article, "The Railroad Crosses the Bay," was written in 2005, when I was serving as executive director of the St. Petersburg Museum of History. The *Journal* has provided a great public service over the past decade. In these times when so much attention is given to the negative, the *Journal* has been a vital positive force bringing focus to our city's special character, as well as the many good people and good things that are here. The *Journal* itself has become a city tradition and positive trendsetter, and I am privileged to be associated with it. I am also appreciative to Arcadia Publishing and The History Press for making my history writings available to a larger audience.

The Making of St. Petersburg focused on fundamental events and turning points in our city's history and how they gave rise to our city's sense of place: the city's creation, the Spanish Entrada, the Great Hurricanes, the Civil War and other topics. This book, *Hidden History of St. Petersburg*, digs deeper and covers aspects of our history that are not as well known or that are newly discovered and chronicled. In several instances, new oral histories add to the stories. For example, an extensive interview is included with Julia Ruth Stevens, Babe Ruth's still vigorous ninety-nine-year-old daughter. Julia was the guest of honor for St. Petersburg's 100th Anniversary of Major League Spring Training, and I had the privilege of escorting her on a tour of the city, which she had not seen since 1943, when she was twenty-six.

At the beginning of this preface is a quote from James S. Baldwin regarding the force of history, written during the civil rights struggle of the 1960s. Baldwin has much to say about the formulation and consequences of history that we can all benefit from and deserves a careful reading. History does influence both present and future. And our understanding of history is a cumulative affair. As years pass, we often obtain a fuller and more complete understanding of earlier events. Sometimes this is the result of new information, and sometimes it is the result of new perspectives.

Much of the material in this book is derived from previous local histories. These particularly include such major works as Karl H. Grismer's *The Story of St. Petersburg* (1948), Walter P. Fuller's *St. Petersburg and Its People* (1972) and Raymond Arsenault's *St. Petersburg and the Florida Dream: 1888–1950* (1988). Dr. Arsenault's work still remains the "Bible" of our local history, and his insights and keen observations are frequently quoted in this effort. For those wishing to read a detailed, comprehensive history, I highly recommend Dr. Arsenault's authoritative and very readable work. Rosalie Peck and Jon Wilson's works have been relied on especially to access the history of our African American community, and Jon Wilson's *The Golden Era in St. Petersburg* is the definitive work on 1950s St. Petersburg. I would be remiss if I did not also mention the work of my friend, the late Scott Taylor Hartzell. Scott in particular made an important contribution to oral history and local biography. Many other works of local history and city documents have been drawn on as well, and also oral histories taken by the St. Petersburg Museum of History's Founding Families Project in which I had the privilege to participate. This book is dedicated to these and other members of St. Petersburg's family of historians.

I also remain deeply grateful to the many people who have helped in one way or another with this work, including the staff at the St. Petersburg Museum of History, especially Ann Wikoff and Marta Jones; the staff at the *Northeast Journal*, particularly Jen MacMillen, Susan Woods Alderson and Julie L. Johnston; Candice Lawrence and Ryan Finn of The History Press; and my wife, Kathy, for her encouragement and assistance with editing.

Special appreciation is given to journalist and historian Jon Wilson for his generous foreword and to Helen Pruitt Wallace, poet laureate of St. Petersburg, for allowing me to include her new work, "Reunion in the Sunshine City." "Reunion" touches on many of the characters and places described in this book, succinctly weaving together much of our city's sense of place.

Most especially, I am thankful to the many people of St. Petersburg who shared their personal histories through interviews, family papers and photos helping to bring new understanding to the history of our great city.

Reunion in the Sunshine City

We are a city of palm trees, banyan, and oak, bougainvillea, hibiscus
and yes, even kudzu twisting its green arms around us. In Williams Park,
Babe Ruth and Peter Demens play checkers through decades;
flying above, Tony Jannus circles and waves. We are a city

of sunlight, beaches, sand, the grand dreams we conjure and failures
we learn from. The well-heeled and homeless, lucky and lost.
We know the cost of neglect—work to fix it. Like Sarah Armistead
in 1913 who once shut saloons like Sunny South, the women

of WCTU, now tap pink toes at the bustling bars on Beach Drive.
Sarah Straub's in the park with her nail file carving her name
in the bark of the Kapok tree, where a mockingbird sings to Bell
Tippetts, who sketches his wing, her parasol tossed on the grass.

The men tip hats as they pass Handsome Jack Taylor sipping
a cold beer at Ferg's. They're all here among us; we are a city
of color, made richer for it: Lakewood, Midtown, Highland Oaks.
The sun shifts every day on all of us; respecting who we're not

shows who we are. This city, like every city learns from scars.
John Donaldson's in 1868, when dark hands paved our streets,
tarred our roofs. Truth is Cooper's Quarters and Pepper Town,
now found in the taste of an orange we peel together. We are a city

of murals blooming on buildings, glittering galleries, children's blue
chalk on our sidewalks, parrots raucous in treetops. And there's Dali
walking his favorite lobster, as Annie McRae paints fishing boats
out on the docks, their nets splayed out like a lady's long tangled hair.

We are a city of lovers that doesn't care if you're gay, straight,
or both. The bay is warm, you can love who you love here.
If you're lucky like Juan Ortiz, that love might save you. He's hugging
Princess Hirrihigua, who freed him in 1536, mounds marking

the spot where they doused him off the spit. We are a city
of laid-back, welcome-back, cool-jack kindness grown thick.
Find us at the Saturday Morning Market, toss Frisbees to our dogs
at the Pier that will one day appear. Even Jack Kerouac's back

reciting his poems, along with Bellona Brown Havens, and wise
Nelson Poynter, pen neatly tucked behind his ear. They're all here
toasting our progress. Doc Webb with his dancing chickens, hailing
brown cigars and sour-sweets, his mermaids waving their green tails.

—Helen Pruitt Wallace, poet laureate of St. Petersburg

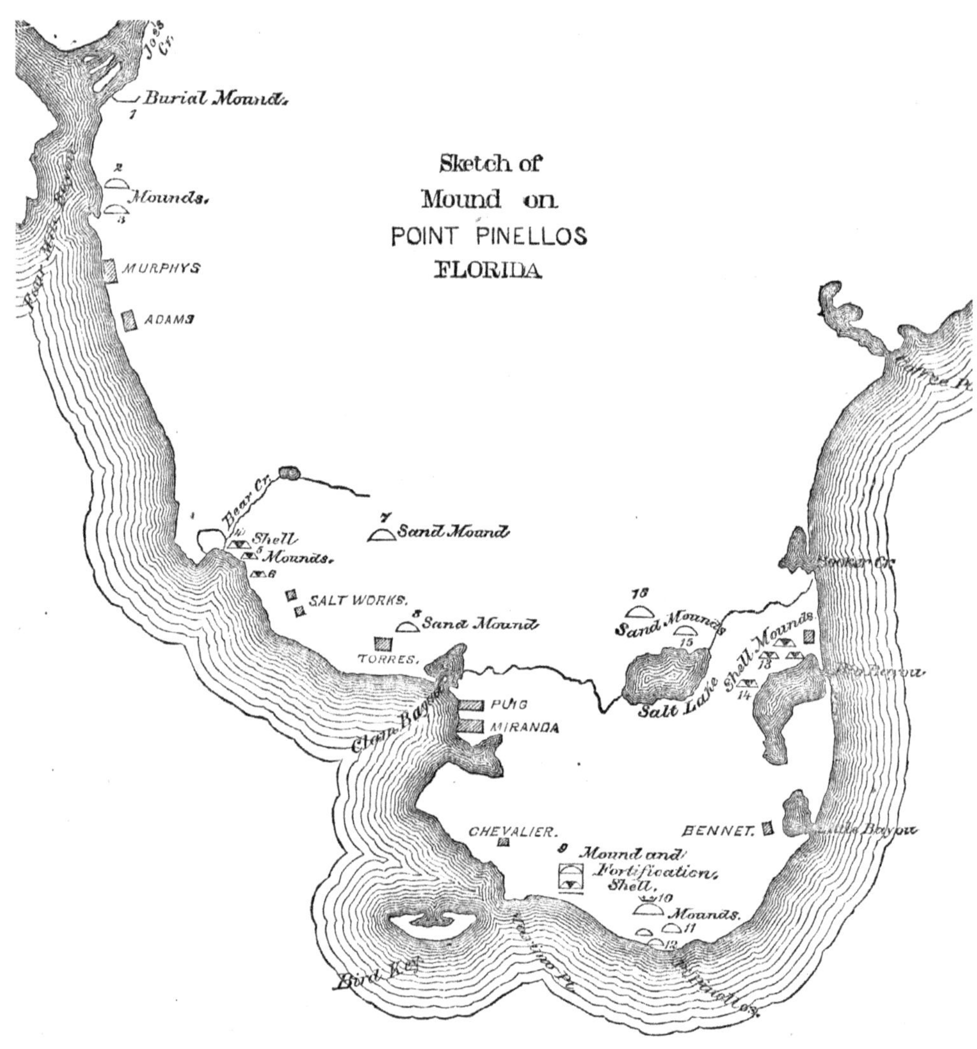

Archaeologist Sylvanus T. Walker's 1879 sketch of Indian mounds located in what was to become St. Petersburg. Mound No. 10 is the Pinellas Point Mound. The "Mound and Fortifications" is the Maximo Point mound site. The dot reading "Chevalier" is the location of notorious bird killer and plume hunter Jean Chevelier's place. *Courtesy Smithsonian Institution,* Annual Report for the Year 1879.

Chapter 1

MAXIMO PARK INDIAN MOUNDS

The St. Petersburg area is rich in archaeological sites. Perhaps the best known is the Weedon Island site at the northeast corner of St. Petersburg facing Tampa Bay. This is the site of the celebrated Weeden Culture dating back to 1000 BCE. (The culture is spelled differently from the island.) Also of note are the Indian mounds on Boca Ciega Bay in the vicinity of Abercrombie Park. But one of the lesser-known sites, part of St. Petersburg's "hidden history," is at the very tip of the southern end of St. Petersburg. This is the site found at Maximo Park. There are two distinct archaeological sites within Maximo Park. One is known as the Maximo Beach Archaeological Site, and the other is known as the Frenchman Creek Archaeological Site. To the east of Maximo Park, on the other side of U.S. 19 and the approach to the Skyway Bridge, is what is known as the Maximo Point Site. And to the east of that is the Pinellas Point Mound.

Archaeological investigations along Maximo Point and Maximo Beach began well before the founding of St. Petersburg. Amateur archaeologist and naturalist Sylvanus T. Walker visited the area in 1879 and wrote a description of his findings for the Smithsonian Institute. Clarence Bloomfield Moore, another celebrated early amateur archaeologist, visited the area in 1900. Archaeologist David Plowden made a field visit in 1952. Others include William Sears of the Florida State Museum (1957), Frank Bushnell (1962), J. Raymond Williams of the University of South Florida (1973), Dudley DeGroot of nearby Eckerd College (1970s), Diane Boyle (1986) and Piper Archaeological Research, which conducted a survey in 1987–88. What attracted all this interest by the archaeological community?

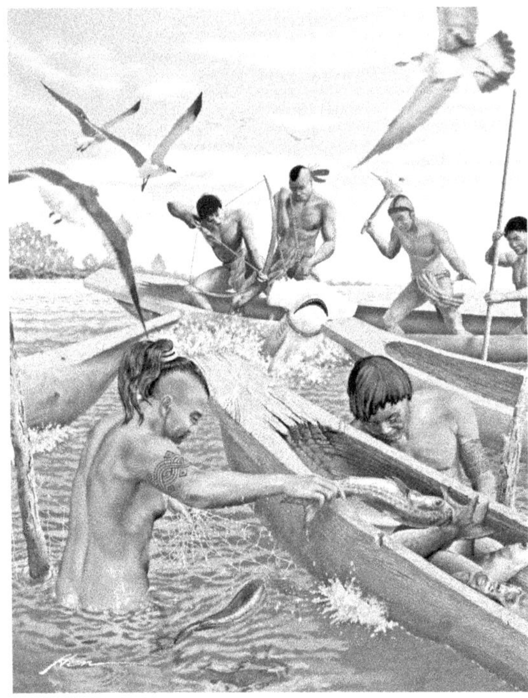

Painting depicting Native American life in the Tampa Bay area. *Courtesy Herman Trappman, artist.*

MAXIMO POINT TEMPLE COMPLEX SITE

The Maximo Point Temple Complex Site is located east of I-275, in the vicinity of 31st Street. That area has been heavily developed in modern times. The site served as a religious and political center for the Safety Harbor cultures, including the Tocobaga Indians, between AD 1000 and AD 1500. Archaeologist Walker's account of the Maximo Point Site described "an immense mound…surrounded by embankments of shell, winding in all directions like modern fortifications." A half mile away from this mound, he reported finding a human skull. The site was occupied during the late Weeden and early Safety Harbor culture periods. Walker also discovered what is now known as the Pinellas Point Mound, located farther east on Mound Place South in the famous "Pink Streets" neighborhood along Tampa Bay at Pinellas Point. This was a "platform" mound, rising at least some sixteen feet. At the time of Walker's examination of the mound, he reported it as twenty-five feet high, although this may have been an error. Originally a shell-and-sand ramp extended south to the bay, where it ended in a shell midden. The ramp was twenty-three feet across and narrowed to twelve feet at the bay. Platform mounds served as the base for public structures and residences of Indian leaders. Walker found various artifacts and some burials there. The Pinellas Point Mound is the best remaining mound in the city and was designated a local landmark in 2003. Concerned because of the site's deterioration after its designation as a landmark, the Greater Pinellas Point Civic Association secured protective measures and a management plan for the site in 2010.

MAXIMO PARK AND BEACH SITE

The Maximo Beach Site is now encompassed by Maximo Park and remains in fair condition. This site is one of the few large shell midden complexes remaining in Florida. It consists of several shell middens (popularly called "kitchen" middens because they are composed of materials used for prehistoric food production and consumption), two large mounds and a submerged midden deposit and lithic scatter (stone tools) located to the

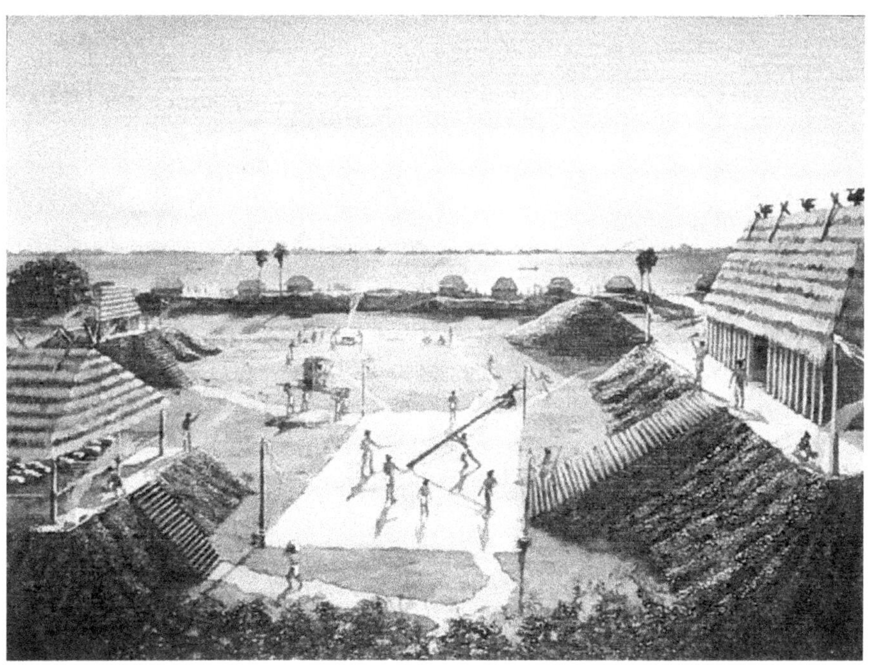

Artist's imagination of Indian Mound complex at Maximo Park. Note the large platform and temple mounds with ramps and plaza, image 2012. *Courtesy City of St. Petersburg/Great Outdoor Publishing Company.*

south beneath the waters of Boca Ciega Bay. The site was occupied during the Middle/Late Archaic through the Spanish contact periods (5000 BCE–AD 1800).

The middens are made up of a variety of shell species, notably whelks and conches. Also found were stone projectile points, shell tools, ceramic fragments and musket balls. Some ceramic fragments date from the Spanish period. To date, no Indian burials have been discovered in the Maximo Beach and Park Site. It was designated a city landmark in 1992, and it is believed to be a part of the larger Maximo Point Temple Complex Site.

FRENCHMAN'S CREEK

While the Maximo Beach and Park Site has been known to archaeologists for many years, the adjacent Frenchman's Creek Site was just recently discovered by archaeologist B.W. Burger. The creek separates the park and Eckerd College on the west and originates out of Loggerhead Marina (formerly Huber Yacht Harbor) to the east. Burger identified two lithic scatters, three shell middens and one early post-Spanish period site. The lithic scatters appear to be Middle/Late Archaic (5000–3000 BCE) and predate the three middens. The middens appear to be late Preceramic Archaic (circa 2000 BCE) and/or "Transitional" (1000–500 BCE). Upon recommendation of archaeologist Burger, the city is seeking to nominate both the new site and the existing park to the National Register of Historic Places.

ANTONIO MAXIMO HERNANDEZ

After the Indians and Spanish, a variety of settlers and entrepreneurs came to what is now St. Petersburg. One was Antonio Maximo Hernandez, after whom Maximo Point and Park is named. He was a fisherman, businessman, guide and landowner. In John A. Bethell's *History of Point Pinellas*, Maximo (in Spanish, paternal family names are listed before maternal) is reported to have been the first "white man" to settle on Pinellas Point, then called *Punta de Pinal* (Point of Pines). Bethell stated that Maximo established a fishery, commonly called a "fish rancho," for supply of the Cuban market in the vicinity of what is now Maximo Park and Maximo Point in 1843. This was done under a land grant from the U.S. government for services he rendered during the Second Seminole War (1835–42). It was the first homestead in Pinellas County. According to historian Walter P. Fuller, Maximo got the land grant after Robert E. Lee came through the Pinellas area during the Second Seminole War. Lee reportedly stated that Maximo was the only person who knew anything about the Seminoles. Lee took Maximo as a scout up the Caloosahatchee River in the vicinity of Fort Myers. Maximo also served as a fishing guide for soldiers at Fort Brooke (Tampa). He resided at Maximo Point until 1848, the year of the Great Hurricane. He either died at Maximo Point shortly before the hurricane or returned to Havana after the hurricane and died. His fish rancho was destroyed. While the property remained in the hands of Maximo's widow, early pioneers Abel Miranda and John and William Bethell again used the site for a fish rancho for a short time before the Civil War.

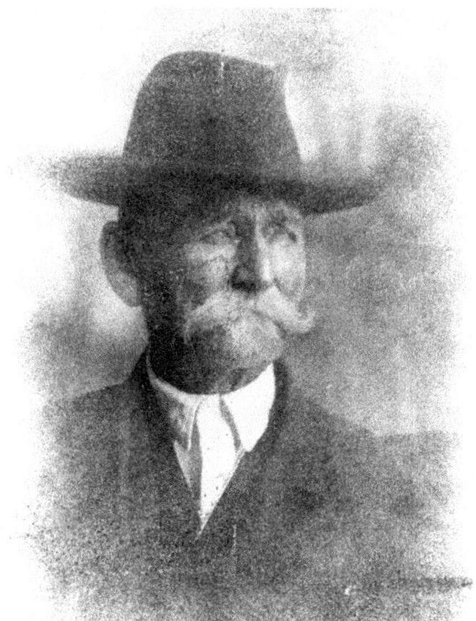

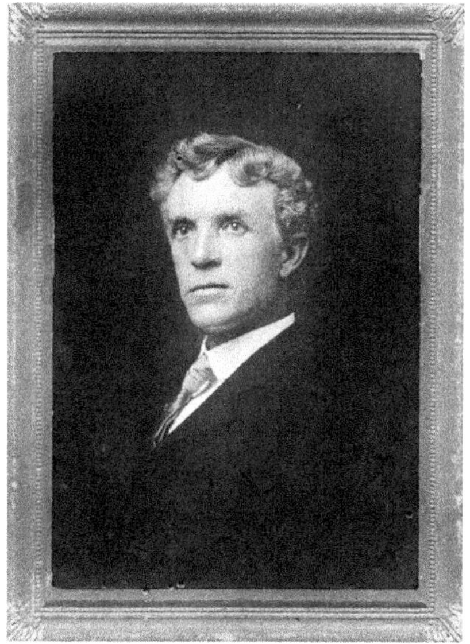

Left: John A. Bethell (1834–1915) was a city pioneer, mercantile businessman, postmaster, justice of the peace and the first city historian, image circa 1914. *Courtesy St. Petersburg Museum of History*.

Right: Roy S. Hanna (1861–1952) was a longtime St. Pete postmaster, noted environmentalist and early organizer of the local Republican Party. Hanna owned Bird Key (originally known as Indian Key) south of Maximo Point. In 1902, he persuaded Theodore Roosevelt to designate Bird Key as a National Bird Sanctuary, image circa 1900. *Courtesy St. Petersburg Museum of History.*

JEAN CHEVELIER

Frenchman's Creek appears to be named for the notorious Jean Chevelier, whose real name was Alfred Lechevelier. In 1880, Chevelier bought the Maximo Point property from Maximo's widow, Dominga. (Archaeologist Sylvanus T. Walker's sketch of Pinellas Point shows Chevelier as already occupying property in the vicinity of Maximo Park in 1879.) Dominga had remarried after Maximo's death, and her new married name was Gomez. Chevelier purported to be a naturalist, but he was actually a plume hunter. At that time plume hunting was immensely profitable. As an example, a snowy egret's fluffy mating feathers fetched thirty-two dollars an ounce—the same as the value of gold. The gular pouches pelicans use to catch fish, also known as "wallets," were made into tobacco pouches. In one season, Chevelier and his workers obtained eleven thousand bird skins and plumes and thirty thousand birds' eggs. Chevelier quickly depopulated the immense bird rookeries that existed at that time in the vicinity of Maximo Point. In about 1882, he moved on to new killing fields in the Everglades near Miami, as well as the Ten Thousand Islands south of Naples. While plume hunting was legal in the late 1800s and hunting in general was common, even some of Chevelier's contemporaries abhorred his decimation of the bird population. John Bethell called Chevelier the "worst scourge that ever came to Pinellas Point."

Dominga originally obtained a land patent to Maximo's property in 1852 but did not record it until 1887. Consequently, she avoided paying taxes on the property for thirty-five years. Apparently, Chevelier never recorded a deed. In 1886, Dominga sold the property again to a group of investors from Baltimore, including Claude Van Bibber, son of the famous Dr. W.C. Van Bibber. It was Dr. Van Bibber who addressed the American Medical Association in 1885 and declared Pinellas Point the healthiest climate in the world, a pronouncement later taken up by early St. Petersburg boosters to sell property and attract new residents and tourists. In his speech, Van Bibber said, "Were I sent abroad for a haven for tired men, where new life would come with every sun, and slumber full of sleep with every moon, I would select Pinellas Point, Florida....Its Indian mounds show that it was selected by the original inhabitants for a popular settlement." As historian Walter Fuller wrote, Dominga "had the distinction of being the first person to hold a valid deed to any land in what is now the city of St. Petersburg, and one of the few to sell the same land twice and avoid unpleasant collision with the law."

After Claude Van Bibber and associates bought the land, it languished and was eventually bought for back taxes. St. Petersburg postmaster Roy

Hanna, who was also a leading city environmentalist, owned the Maximo property for a time. He also owned nearby Bird Key (originally called Indian Key), which he donated to the federal government as a national bird sanctuary in about 1902. The Maximo property eventually ended up in possession of the city, which used it for O'Neill's Marina, Eckerd College and Maximo Park. For a time, Maximo Park beach was one of two city beaches used by African Americans during the era of segregation.

Many Native Americans view the mounds as cultural or ancestral sites that may be part of an active religious system that should remain undisturbed. The Florida Miccosukee tribe, for example, believes that "what is in the ground should remain in the ground." They believe that human and other remains were placed in the ground by spiritual forces. The Maximo mound sites are presently occupied by homes, parks, a wilderness preserve, docks for fishing, boats, a college and a few protected vestiges of the mounds themselves. The city recently expanded the boundaries of the archaeological site at the park and is considering additional measures to protect the park's mounds. It is also considering making Maximo Park a new site for community education and heritage tourism, including an interpretive center. What would the former Native American inhabitants think of their Maximo home today?

Sources: Raymond Arsenault, *St. Petersburg and the Florida Dream: 1888–1950* (1988/96); John A. Bethell, *Bethell's History of Point Pinellas* (1914/62); City of St. Petersburg, "Historic Designation Staff Report," HPC #91-05; City of St. Petersburg, "Staff Report (Maximo Archaeological Site)," CPC Case No. 11-90200051, 1991; City of St. Petersburg, "Staff Report," HPC 12-90300002, 2012; City of St. Petersburg, draft, "Maximo Park Master Plan," 2012; Jack E. Davis, *An Everglades Providence: Marjory Stoneman Douglas and the American Environmental Century* (2009); Hampton Dunn, *Yesterday's St. Petersburg* (1973); Karl H. Grismer, *The Story of St. Petersburg* (1948); Walter P. Fuller, *St. Petersburg and Its People* (1972); Walter P. Fuller, "Who Was the Frenchman of Frenchman's Creek?" (no date); Jannus Research, "Pinellas Point Indian Mound Archaeological Management Plan," prepared for City of St. Petersburg Parks Department, 2010; Gerry Lempke, "Maximo Road, a/k/a 31st St. S." (2006); I. Mac Perry, *Indian Mounds You Can Visit* (1993); Smithsonian Institution, *Annual Report for the Year 1879* (1880); R. Bruce Stephenson, *Visions of Eden* (1997); and communications with Harry Piper and Jeff Moates.

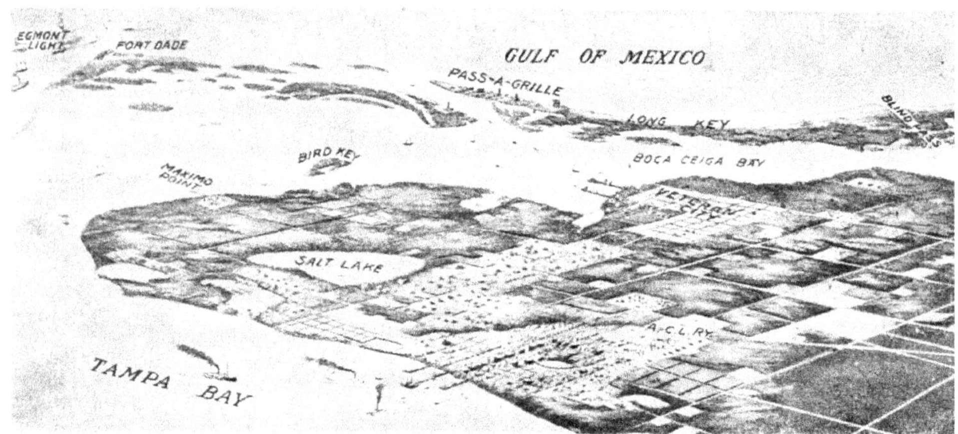

A 1909 pictorial map postcard of St. Petersburg and South Pinellas. Note Salt Lake (now Lake Maggiore), Maximo Point, Bird Key and Veteran City (now Gulfport). Fort Dade is shown where what is known today as Fort De Soto is located. Originally, Fort Dade encompassed both Egmont and Mullet Keys, but in 1900, Mullet Key was designated Fort De Soto. *Courtesy Michaels Family Collection.*

Chapter 2

The Detroit

Queen Mother of Our Hotels

There is no more historic building in St. Petersburg than the Detroit Hotel. Located on the historic 200 block of Central Avenue, sometimes referred to as the "First Block," the hotel was built in 1888 by Peter Demens, one of St. Petersburg's three founders. It was Peter Demens who brought the railroad, sparking the city's creation. Without the railroad, St. Petersburg would never have happened as we know it.

The two other founders were General John Constantine Williams, and Williams's wife, Sarah. Sarah Williams negotiated with Peter Demens's assistant Henry Sweetapple to bring the railroad in exchange for land provided by her husband, John. There is the famous story about John Williams and Peter Demens flipping a silver half dollar to see who would get to name the new town. Supposedly, Demens won and named the town after his hometown, St. Petersburg, Russia. Williams got to name the hotel after his hometown, Detroit. The real story was far less dramatic. The local postmistress went to one of Demens's other assistants, Joseph Henschen, and asked what the new town should be named. Henschen said that Mr. Demens always wanted to name a town after his hometown of St. Petersburg, and so it was done. Actually, Demens had planned to name the town St. Petersburg before the postmistress's meeting with Henschen. There is both a letter written by Demens and a map using the name St. Petersburg that predate their meeting.

The original deal between Williams and Demens did not include building a hotel. This was later added by Demens. Williams contributed $5,000 toward the cost of the construction, with Demens and the railway picking up the rest, for a total cost of approximately $10,000. The hotel was intended to help jump-start development of the city and use of Demens's Orange Belt Railway. By the end of 1888, the forty-room, three-and-a-half-story-high hotel was complete, including a seventy-foot tower. The hotel also later boasted the oldest elevator on the west coast of Florida.

There the hotel stood, virtually in the middle of nowhere, beckoning the tourist and developers to come—by railroad, of course. As late as 1901, hotel guests could delight in deer that sheltered in nearby trees. Starting in July 1889, the Orange Belt Railway sponsored seaside tours to exotic and healthful St. Petersburg. Advertisements in northern newspapers featured the Detroit Hotel along with Dr. W.C. Van Bibber's famous 1885 report declaring St. Petersburg's climate as the healthiest in the world. Demens also added a bathing pavilion at his railroad pier to further entice visitors.

A little-known fact is that the hotel's first tenants were African American railroad laborers who worked for Peter Demens. The hotel served as a rooming house for the workers, who moved to it from their tents and shacks. It originally also served as an on-site branch office of the Orange Belt Railroad. Its first manager was E.G. Peyton from Virginia.

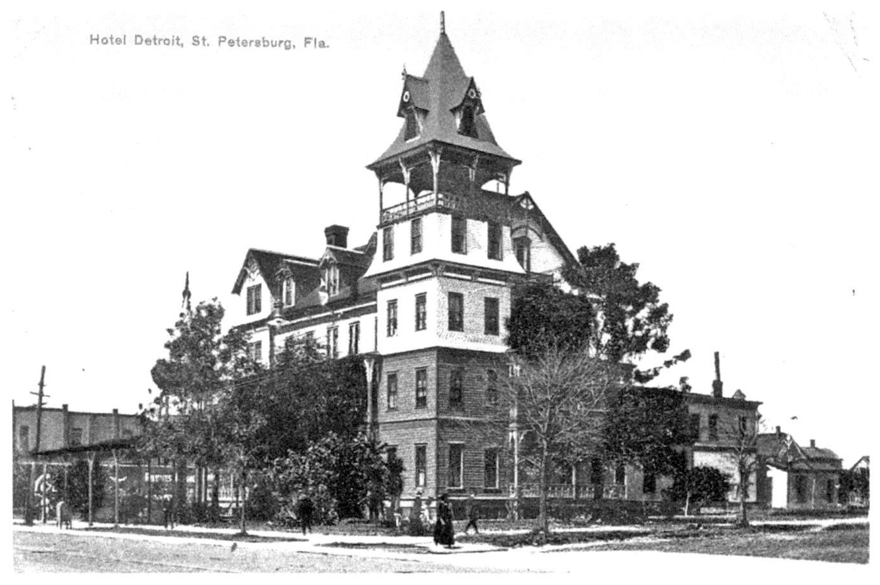

Early postcard depicting the Detroit Hotel, image circa 1900. *Courtesy Michaels Family Collection.*

Historian Karl Grismer, who knew of the hotel firsthand from the 1920s, declared the hotel "as fine a hotel as could be found…in any resort city on the Florida West Coast." The hotel, like the nearby Orange Belt Railway depot, was built in a Russian style. It was constructed of the best woods. A gazebo with a distinct minaret was added in the late 1890s. A west wing was added in about 1911. In 1913, a sixty-room brick addition was added to the east. In 1901, an eighty-dollar bronze fountain was installed on the corner of the Detroit Hotel grounds by the Loyal Christian Temperance Union to promote temperance. The water was cooled by ice stored in a box in the foundation of the fountain.

There is a story that soon after the hotel was built, Peter Demens and his Russian associates went there for dinner. The first course was extremely hot soup. Upon taking a sip, Demens spit it out. His Russian associates thought it was an American custom, so they spit their soup out, too. In truth, his associates were not Russian. One was a Swede (Henschen), one a Canadian (Sweetapple) and one an American (A.M. Taylor). But it's a good story.

HURRICANE OF 1921

The Detroit survived the "Big One" in 1921, though not without paying a price. Historian Walter P. Fuller was staying at the Detroit on the day St. Petersburg's only hurricane hit. He awoke at three o'clock in the morning to find wind and water coming into his room. He then left to serve as a Red Cross volunteer. Later, he returned to his room to try to get some sleep. Upon awaking, he found the roof above him gone. But the hurricane was not big enough to put the Detroit out of business. In fact, the city's leading citizens gathered there after the storm to plan recovery, including pledging $20,000 to rebuild the Municipal Pier. The pier was rebuilt in a mere two months. Mary Brazier, who was associated with the hotel from 1940 to 1969, remembered when later hurricanes would threaten, neighbors gathered in the hotel lobby for safety.

Hotel Owners

The hotel's owners have included such city legends as C. Perry Snell, Frank Fortune Pulver and Hubert Rutland. Snell is known as the "Father of St. Petersburg's Parks." He also gave the city its Mediterranean Revival "look" beginning in 1924. Pulver was the city's "millionaire bachelor mayor." He made his fortune developing a chewing gum dispenser and a popular brand of spearmint gum. He later sold out to William Wrigley Jr. of Wrigley Chewing Gum. Pulver teamed up with city publicity director John Lodwick to give the city its zany side. Dressed in white from head to toe, Mayor Pulver walked down Broadway in New York City with a bevy of St. Petersburg beauty queens. He also, tongue in cheek, appointed himself the city's "Bathing Suit Inspector." "Women's bathing suits were required to cover at least half their bodies." He was photographed meticulously measuring them with a ruler. All this was done to draw the tourist dollar to St. Pete. In the 1920s, St. Petersburg was thought by many throughout the nation to be a town of "beautiful women and their grandparents." Hubert Rutland was a longtime banker and merchant. Rutland Brothers Department Store graced Central Avenue for many years. His handsome estate can still be seen on Little Bayou at Sunrise Drive, near 51st Avenue, in South St. Pete.

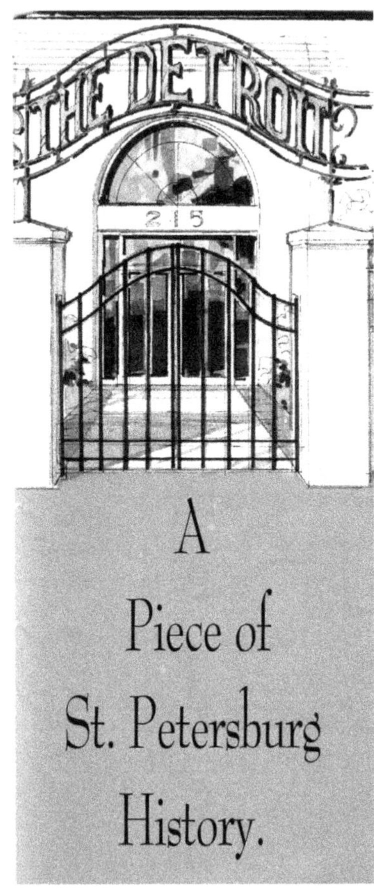

Brochure used to promote sale of condos in the Historic Detroit Hotel. *Courtesy Michaels Family Collection.*

The Detroit Hotel was also the birthplace of one of the town's most productive associations: the Woman's Town Improvement Association (WTIA). On May 7, 1901, the women called a meeting at the Detroit, and the association was formed. The association's charter called for city beautification, advancing the welfare of St. Petersburg's citizens and providing for the entertainment and comfort of visitors and tourists.

MARY BRAZIER REMEMBERS

Mary Brazier remembered growing up at the Detroit. Her parents, uncle and great-aunt, Ida Nancy Merrill, owned the Detroit from 1940 to 1969. Her father was Frank Brazier, and her mother was Isabelle Kelly Brazier. Her uncle was Charles Brazier. Mary visited the hotel on holidays and during the summers from 1940 until she moved to St. Petersburg in 1954. She helped out at the front desk and in many other ways. She remembered as a young girl the sailors who stayed at the hotel during World War II. "The hotel had boarded up fire places and lots of secret places." Also included in the hotel at that time was the "One Hundred Hall," originally leased from the 1920s commercial building directly behind the Detroit at 200–206 1st Avenue North. At the time, Hubert Rutland owned this building. This building still remains and retains the original storefronts, canopy and wire-cut brick detailing. Between the Detroit Hotel proper and the Rutland annex, the hotel had a total of 233 rooms. Rooms in the Hundred Hall rented for $1.50 per night. Those in the hotel proper ranged from $2.50 to $5.00. The Hundred Hall did not have private baths. Rooms in the east wing of the hotel proper had water views.

The train station was a block away from the hotel. A porter was sent to greet the arriving hotel guests and escort them to the hotel. Mary remembered the guests as mostly elderly women. Mary's cousin also stayed at the hotel. She had a pet alligator. As the alligator grew in size, "it was not loved by the guests." She remembered the hotel dining room as "quite elegant with white table clothes and bent wood chairs." The formal hotel restaurant was later succeeded by the Patio restaurant and, later, the Garden Restaurant. Emmanuel Roux operated the Garden Restaurant for many years beginning in the early 1990s. He tried to keep the restaurant décor in keeping with the hotel's traditional style. One of his patrons was Ringo Starr.

In about 1959, Mary's parents took out a mortgage to rewire the hotel for air conditioning. Locals used to come and sit in the lobby just to get out of the summer heat. Every Christmas and New Year's, there was a big party. A ten-foot-tall Christmas tree stood in the corner of the lobby. Santa would be there on Christmas. It was Mary's job to present a gift to each guest. Many clubs had their meetings at the Detroit. Among these were the Rotary Club, the Zonta Business Women's Club and the Young Republican Club.

MRS. FRANKLIN D. ROOSEVELT
55 EAST 74TH STREET
NEW YORK CITY 21, N. Y.

March 14, 1960

Dear Miss Merrill:

This is a note to thank you warmly for your very kind welcome to the Detroit Hotel. The flowers were lovely and I enjoyed my brief stay in your pleasant hotel.

I would just like to say that I especially appreciated your note with the flowers. It amused and pleased me.

With every good wish,

Very sincerely yours,

Eleanor Roosevelt

Letter sent by Eleanor Roosevelt to Ida Nancy Merrill, owner of the Detroit from 1940 to 1969. Although Ida Merrill was a staunch Republican, she and Eleanor got along well. Eleanor was in the city to address Gibbs College. Her speech was interrupted by a bomb scare, image 1960. *Courtesy Mary Brazier.*

Mary remembered two guests in particular. One was John F. Kennedy. He attended a ten-dollar-per-plate dinner at the Detroit while campaigning for president in 1959. Mary stood at the hotel entrance canopy as Kennedy passed by with his bodyguards. She remembered he was very handsome, and she was disappointed that Jackie was not with him. Somebody, in fact, asked if she were Jackie! She also remembered that Eleanor Roosevelt stayed at the hotel in 1960. Mrs. Roosevelt and Mary's great-aunt, Ida Merrill, "hit it off quite well" in spite of the fact that Ida was a staunch Republican. Eleanor was in the city to make a speech at Gibbs College (now high school). There was a bomb scare during her address, and she refused to leave until everyone else did. After the building was cleared, she continued with her talk but first noted, "If I am blown up by your bomber of racism, that will not change a thing. The inevitable is going to happen. I think it is shameful that the Negro must carry out this process to obtain his civil rights."

In earlier times, the hotel had a steady stream of guest celebrities. Some of these included presidential candidate and later secretary of state William Jennings Bryan, Babe Ruth, the humorist Will Rogers and Clarence Darrow, Bryan's lawyer-opponent in the famous Scopes Monkey Trial. The St. Louis Cardinals also stayed there. Emmanuel Roux, owner of the Detroit Garden Restaurant, noted that he heard many customer accounts regarding

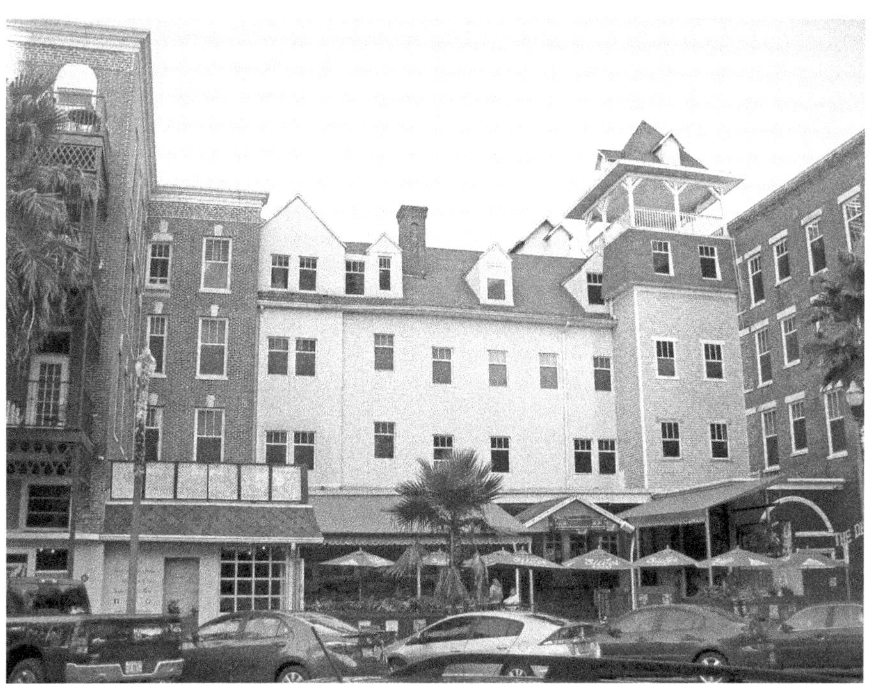

Photo of the Historic Detroit Hotel as it looks today. The original hotel is somewhat hidden between the two brick wings added in 1911 and 1913. The gabled dormers and decorative brick chimney are original to the structure. The tower was rebuilt in 2002. *Courtesy Michaels Family Collection.*

Jim Morrison of the Doors performing at the Detroit before he achieved international fame as a rock star. Morrison attended St. Petersburg Junior College in 1961–62 and performed frequently at the Beaux Arts Gallery in nearby Pinellas Park. The Braziers sold the hotel in 1968 to E.B. Porter, William R. Canning and Harold E. Wells.

Mary Brazier graduated from St. Petersburg High School and, later, from the University of South Florida. She worked for seven years in Germany with the Central Intelligence Agency. Later, she was a trust officer and vice-president of Sun Trust Bank and then worked as the development officer for the Westminster Retirement Communities.

QUEEN MOTHER OF HOTELS

Before the Vinoy, there was the Detroit. As the "Queen Mother" of St. Petersburg's hotels, it paved the way for the city's tourist economy and development. At the beginning of the 1920s, St. Petersburg only had five hotels, led by the Detroit. But in the '20s, the hotel business exploded with such additions as the Ponce de Leon, the Soreno, the Suwanee, the Pheil, the Princess Martha, the Pennsylvania, the Dennis, the Vinoy Park, the Jungle Country Club, the Rolyat and, finally, the Don CeSar. Hotels and St. Petersburg's growth have gone hand in hand since the very beginning. Without the hotels, St. Petersburg's tourist and development economy would not have happened. While the hotels themselves provided employment to thousands of local residents, more importantly, they provided employment for a great many others working in a wide range of other local business enterprises also patronized by tourists. It was the Detroit Hotel that led the way in development of the city and the tourist economy for which it is so famous. For many years, it served as an important city social and cultural center.

The Detroit no longer serves as a hotel. Its upper floors have been converted into condominiums, and Jannus Landing, one of St. Pete's most lively music venues, is situated on the north side of the hotel, where utilities were once located. The Queen Mother of hotels was designated a local landmark in 2010 thanks to the leadership of Saint Petersburg Preservation, as well as help from the city's mayor, Bill Foster; the city council; and widespread community support. The Detroit is a good example of a historic building continuing to meet important community needs.

Sources: Raymond Arsenault, *St. Petersburg and the Florida Dream: 1888–1950* (1988/96); City of St. Petersburg, "Staff Report," HPC 09-04/09-9030006, 2010; *Evening Independent*, February 17, 1979; Scott Hartzell, *St. Petersburg: An Oral History* (2002); Karl H. Grismer, *Story of St. Petersburg* (1948); Rick Baker, *Mangroves to Major League* (2000); Arden Moore, "The Twelve Lost Colleges of Florida," *Sun Sentinel*, February 12, 1995; Albert Parry, *Full Steam Ahead! The Story of Peter Demens, Founder of St. Petersburg, Florida* (1987); *St. Petersburg Times*, various dates but especially August 19, 1974; *Sun Sentinel*, February 12, 1995; the Garden Restaurant, "The Detroit Legacy"; Dean Brazier, "St. Petersburg: The Way It Was" (manuscript); State University System of Florida, Sanborn Maps Collection; and interview with Mary Brazier.

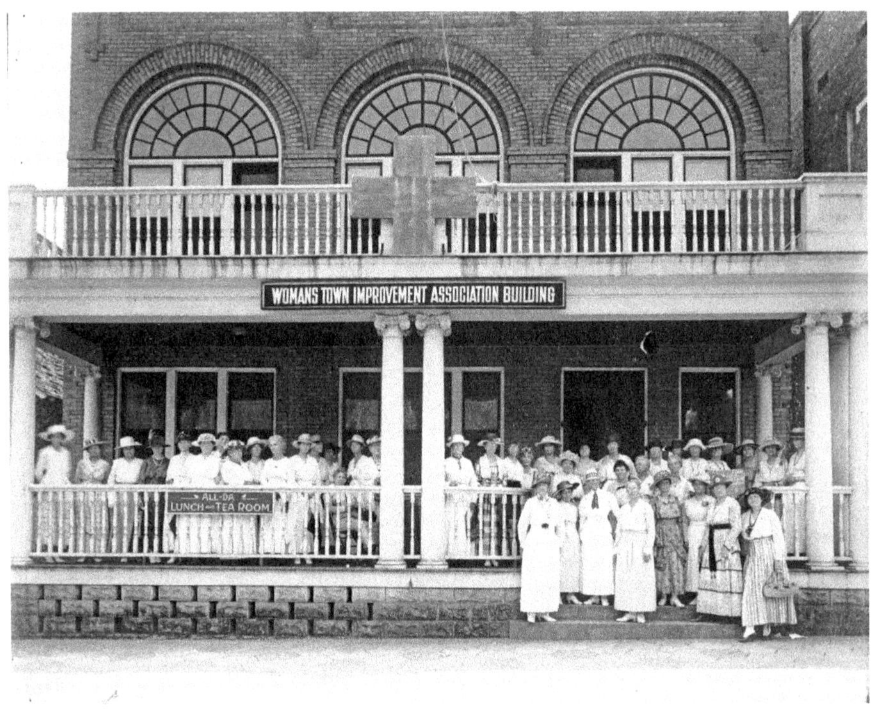

Woman's Town Improvement Association members pose for photo in front of the headquarters they built facing Williams Park in 1913 at a cost of $20,000. The building is now a city landmark, image 1913. *Courtesy St. Petersburg Museum of History.*

Chapter 3

MEDDLERS OR VISIONARIES?

The Woman's Town Improvement Association

Described by historian Walter P. Fuller as "the matriarch of all clubs in St. Petersburg" and "the fountainhead of most of the principal cultural, civic and public social activities of the city," the Woman's Town Improvement Association (WTIA) was founded in May 1901 at the Detroit Hotel. It was an outgrowth of a local park improvement organization dating back to 1888, the year St. Petersburg itself was founded. The association's charter called for city beautification, advancing the welfare of St. Petersburg's citizens and providing for the entertainment and comfort of visitors and tourists. With the help of city benefactor Edwin Tomlinson, the WTIA initiated the city's Washington Birthday parades that eventually evolved into today's Festival of the States Parade and sponsored Lyceum courses and Chautauqua lectures. It advocated for parks, sidewalks, band shells, paved streets, animal control, prison reform (including the city's first probation program), abolition of the convict lease system and wildlife preservation. The association lobbied to preserve the Indian shell mound at Mound Park, near today's Bayfront Hospital. Prior to the establishment of a hospital, it helped establish a "Poor-Sick" fund that provided the poor with medications. It petitioned Congress for better films, particularly for African American children. The association even pushed for immigration reform.

The WTIA was composed of the community's most prominent society women. Its first president was Isabelle Weller, wife of Arthur P. Weller. Weller was a cousin of F.A. Davis, who brought electricity and the trolleys to St. Petersburg. Weller was also manager of Davis's electric power plant on the waterfront. Another prominent WTIA member was Sarah Williams Armistead. First married to "General" John Constantine Williams Sr. and, later, to Mayor James Armistead, she was also an activist in the Woman's Christian Temperance Union. Along with her first husband, John, and the railroad entrepreneur Peter Demens, she is considered by many to also be a city founder. She played a central role in negotiating the agreement bringing the Orange Belt Railway to St. Petersburg. More than any other event, it was the coming of the railroad that created St. Petersburg.

Isabelle Weller was succeeded as president by Sarah Moore Straub. Sarah was the wife of William L. Straub, owner and publisher of the *St. Petersburg Times*. Another prominent member was Katherine Bell Tippetts, founder of the St. Petersburg Audubon Society and the person responsible for having the mocking bird declared Florida's state bird.

The WTIA's greatest leader was Mary Merrell, wife of a well-known real estate broker and attorney. She served first as association president in 1912 and then again from 1921 to 1929. Originally, WTIA meetings were held in hotels or at members' homes. Meetings were begun with the Lord's Prayer, and latecomers were fined. Under Merrell's stewardship, the WTIA built its own building in 1913 at a cost of $20,000. The Neoclassical-style, two-story building was designed by M.E. Benjamin and constructed by H.W. Plunkett. It was located at 326 1st Avenue North, facing Williams Park. During World War I, the building was used by the Red Cross. Later, it was given by the WTIA to the YWCA. It still stands today, adjacent to the Dennis Hotel (now called Williams Park Hotel). In 1998, the WTIA Building was designated a historical site. Significantly, the building was originally shared with the Board of Trade. Historian Raymond Arsenault wrote, "This unusual arrangement disturbed and embarrassed some members of the local male elite, but anyone who lived in the city for any length of time knew that it was not easy to keep up with the 'meddling women' of the WTIA."

The organization's initial activities included the beautification of Williams Park with magnolias, oaks and date palms. Association women did the plantings and gardening themselves. These were all-day affairs that included picnic lunches. Mary Merrell later recalled, "Little by little, Williams Park became a place of beauty. Walks were installed, a fountain installed in the center, and benches scattered about."

In 1910, the WTIA, closely allied with the Woman's Christian Temperance Union, backed local church efforts to rid the community of gamblers, drunkards and cigarette smokers. It advocated for a "blue law" that would prohibit local stores from opening on Sunday and actually got the city council to draft such an ordinance. However, this created such an outcry in the business community that the draft was withdrawn at the next meeting. Historian Arsenault observed, "Such attempts to return the community to moral rectitude sometimes pitted the women of the WTIA against husbands, fathers, and sons, and perhaps a few daughters as well, but the Victorian gentility of the organization generally prevented all-out conflict."

Perhaps the WTIA's least appreciated but most important contribution to our city was its support of William Straub's crusade to preserve the waterfront as parkland. This was accomplished in 1909. The presence of Sarah Straub in the association was no doubt a major factor. Waterfront acquisition was also advocated by the Board of Trade. Acquisition of the waterfront for public use is seen by many historians as the most important turning point in St. Petersburg's history.

Ellen Babb, education curator at Heritage Village in Largo, where many local historic buildings are preserved, described the members of the WTIA as "progressive women who came from the North and brought with them the ideas of that area—temperance, anti-smoking, and anti-child labor. They were similar to today's League of Women Voters…these women dispelled the Victorian stereotype of housewives who were publicly and economically impotent." The Woman's Town Improvement Association was finally dissolved in 1934, after other groups, such as the Junior League, assumed many of its concerns. The association left a legacy of compassion, civic responsibility and vision that serves as a model for the city yet today.

Sources: Raymond Arsenault, *St. Petersburg and the Florida Dream: 1888–1950* (1988/1996); Walter P. Fuller, *St. Petersburg and Its People* (1972); Scott Taylor Hartzell, *St. Petersburg: An Oral History* (2002); Karl H. Grismer, *The Story of St. Petersburg* (1948); and the St. Petersburg Museum of History.

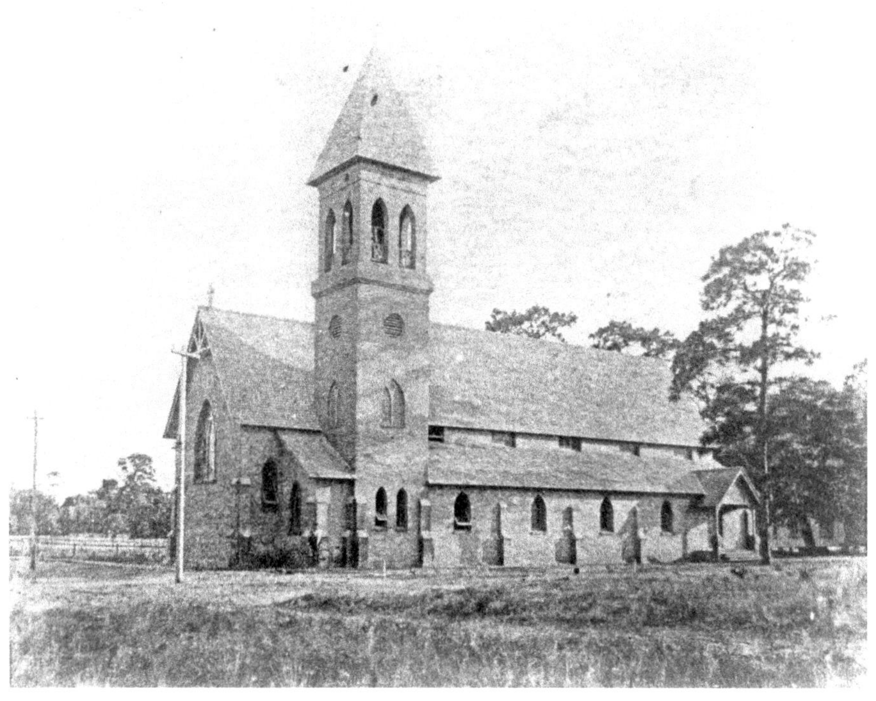

Very early photo of St. Peter's Cathedral Church. The rectory has not yet been built. Obscured building at the right may be the original Mission of the Holy Spirit, image circa 1908. *Courtesy St. Petersburg Museum of History.*

Chapter 4

St. Peter's Cathedral Church

One of our city's greatest unsung treasures is St. Peter's Episcopal Cathedral Church. The cathedral was built in the tradition of Late Gothic Revival–style architecture, popularly known locally as "Florida Gothic." The building dates from 1899, only eleven years after our city's founding. St. Peter's Church as an organization dates from 1889. The history of St. Peter's is intertwined with the history of the city itself.

South Pinellas County's early pioneers, many of them with English roots, founded St. Petersburg's Episcopal community. The oldest church of any denomination in what is now St. Petersburg is St. Bartholomew's Church. St. Bartholomew's is also an Episcopal church and was built in 1887 at what is now 22nd Avenue and 18th Street South. The church cemetery still remains there, but the church itself was relocated to 38th Avenue and 34th Street South in 1970. Once St. Bartholomew's was established, according to the St. Peter's Church Secretary's Book, it built a new chapel in 1889 known as the Mission of the Holy Spirit. This was located in the new town of St. Petersburg on 11th Street between 5th Avenue and Baum Avenue North. Baum Avenue was named after Jacob Baum, a church member and benefactor, who donated the land for the new mission according to church minutes. (Some other secondary accounts state that the land was "purchased from and partly donated by" the St. Petersburg Land and Improvement Company, successor to the Orange Belt [Railway] Investment Company.)

But St. Peter's Church's greatest benefactor was Edwin Hyde Tomlinson. Tomlinson was also the city's greatest benefactor. A native of Connecticut, his first documented visit to St. Petersburg was in 1891, and he moved to the city permanently in 1896. He made his fortune in mining, oil and agriculture. Wasting no time, he immediately set about to leave his stamp on the city. In partnership with the Woman's Town Improvement Association, he organized Washington Birthday celebrations and festivals that eventually evolved into today's Festival of the States Parade. He outfitted a student band with instruments. He built and donated the Domestic and Manual Training School (1901), Florida's first, to the local school system. This building still stands as the city hall annex located between St. Peter's and today's city hall and is designated a local landmark. In 1902, he built the Manual Training Annex at 4th Street and 1st Avenue South with a 2,500-seat auditorium for use by students and the public. The capacity of this building was remarkable considering the city's population was only 1,575 persons in 1900. A year later, the annex became the city hall. It was also called the Tomlinson Armory Building. He paid for the city's first Open-Air Post Office (1905) on the very site of the current Open-Air Post Office. Together with another local resident, he built the city's first hospital, Augusta Memorial, named after his mother. This eventually evolved into present-day Bayfront Hospital. He built a pier at the foot of 3rd Avenue South that included an artesian well that later became the famous Fountain of Youth. There is a monument to the Fountain of Youth (complete with fountain) at 4th Avenue and 1st Street Southeast. He donated the land for the city's first electric plant, now the site of the Yacht Club. He was also a generous supporter of the Boy Scouts, the YMCA and the American Legion. Tomlinson met Guglielmo Marconi while traveling in Italy and later built a two-hundred-foot tower on his St. Petersburg residence for Marconi to test his radio experiments. Marconi never came.

Not the least of Tomlinson's largess was his support of St. Peter's Church. In 1896, Edwin Tomlinson donated land for a better site for the Episcopal Church at the corner of 2nd Avenue and 4th Street North across from Williams Park in honor of his father, Peter Tomlinson, who resided with him in St. Pete. After Edwin Tomlinson donated the land at 2nd and 4th, the Mission of the Holy Spirit Chapel was moved to the new site and its name changed to St. Peter's Church. In 1899, a further donation was made of adjacent property and $5,000 toward the building of a new brick church to replace the old chapel building. Work on the new church building was completed about that same year.

In 1901, another $2,000 was donated for a rectory. The earliest published history of the founding of St. Peter's is Karl H. Grismer's *History of St.*

Petersburg (1924). Grismer unequivocally stated that Edwin Tomlinson built both the church and the rectory and that he "bore all expense." Church records, however, indicate that church members subscribed to a new building fund in 1893. Whether this was also applied to the new church is uncertain. A 1966 *St. Petersburg Times* article appears to note that Archdeacon John H. Weddell was the architect of the original church building (the text is somewhat unclear). The article also states that the contractor was David Ferdon. Ferdon was St. Petersburg's first professional architect and not a contractor, although it is possible he may have acted in the capacity of a contractor at times. Any association with St. Peter's was more likely in the role of architect. Additionally, an association with the original church building is questionable, as he did not permanently move to the city until 1903, although it is known that he designed at least one notable building before 1899. It is more likely that Charles F. May was the contractor for the church. May did contracting for Edwin Tomlinson about this time, including building the Domestic and Manual Training School adjacent to St. Peter's. Interestingly, the bricks used in the Training School are the same as those used in St. Peter's. They are a sand brick made in north Florida. After the new church was built, the chapel then was used as a parish hall until sometime between 1904 and 1908, when it was moved to make way for a new parish hall, which was completed about 1910.

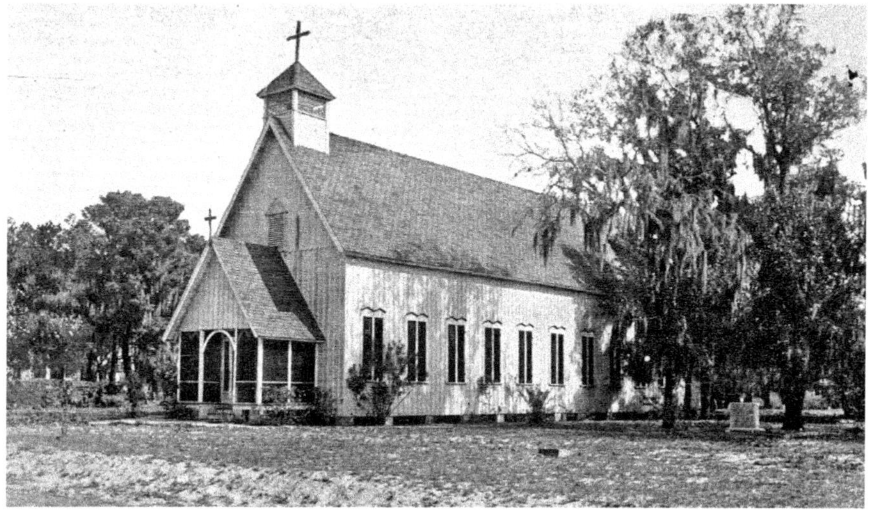

St. Bartholomew's Church was the first church built in what is now St. Petersburg and dates from 1887. The church was originally built on 22nd Avenue South, also called Lakeview Avenue. It was later moved to 34th Street and 38th Avenue South, where it still flourishes today. *Courtesy Michaels Family Collection.*

In 1914, the church's principal stained-glass window of "Christ Walking on Water" was donated and erected by the Tomlinson family in honor of Reverend Charles McIlvaine Gray, who served St. Peter's from 1902 to until his death in 1911. Reverend Gray is buried at St. Bartholomew's cemetery. In 1940, the old parish hall and rectory were replaced with a new parish hall south of the church designed by architect William B. Harvard, a church member. This was attached to the sanctuary by sidewalks with a covered roof. In 1958–59, Harvard designed an addition to the parish hall used as a Sunday school. All of this was demolished in 2008 to make way for a new multipurpose building.

It is not certain how St. Peter's got its name. The church may be named after the city that Edwin Tomlinson loved. The fact that Saint Peter was a fisherman, and that St. Petersburg was at that time in large part a commercial fishing center, may also have something to do with it. On the lighter side, some have observed that Tomlinson made his donations in honor of his father, Peter, and perhaps he was the "Saint" referenced. Perhaps all three of these considerations merged to suggest the name.

St. Peter's was not the first church in the new city. Other early churches included the Congregational Church, formally organized into the United Church of Christ in 1888. Its members held services for three years before it was formally organized at the Miranda Schoolhouse at Maximo Point. After its organization, services were first held in a passenger car at the Orange Belt Railway Station. The First Methodist Church was also organized in

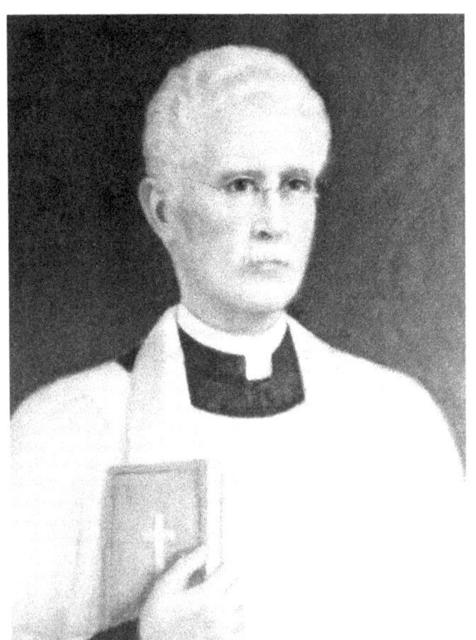

Opposite: How St. Peter's Cathedral Church got its name is uncertain. In this rare early postcard, St. Peter extends a "hearty welcome" to the city, image circa 1930. *Gulf Coast Card Company, St. Petersburg & Curt Tech & Company Inc., Chicago; courtesy Michaels Family Collection.*

Left: Reverend Charles McIlvaine Gray served St. Peter's from 1902 to until his death in 1911. The great stained-glass window behind the altar was donated in his honor by the Tomlinson family. *Courtesy St. Peter's Cathedral.*

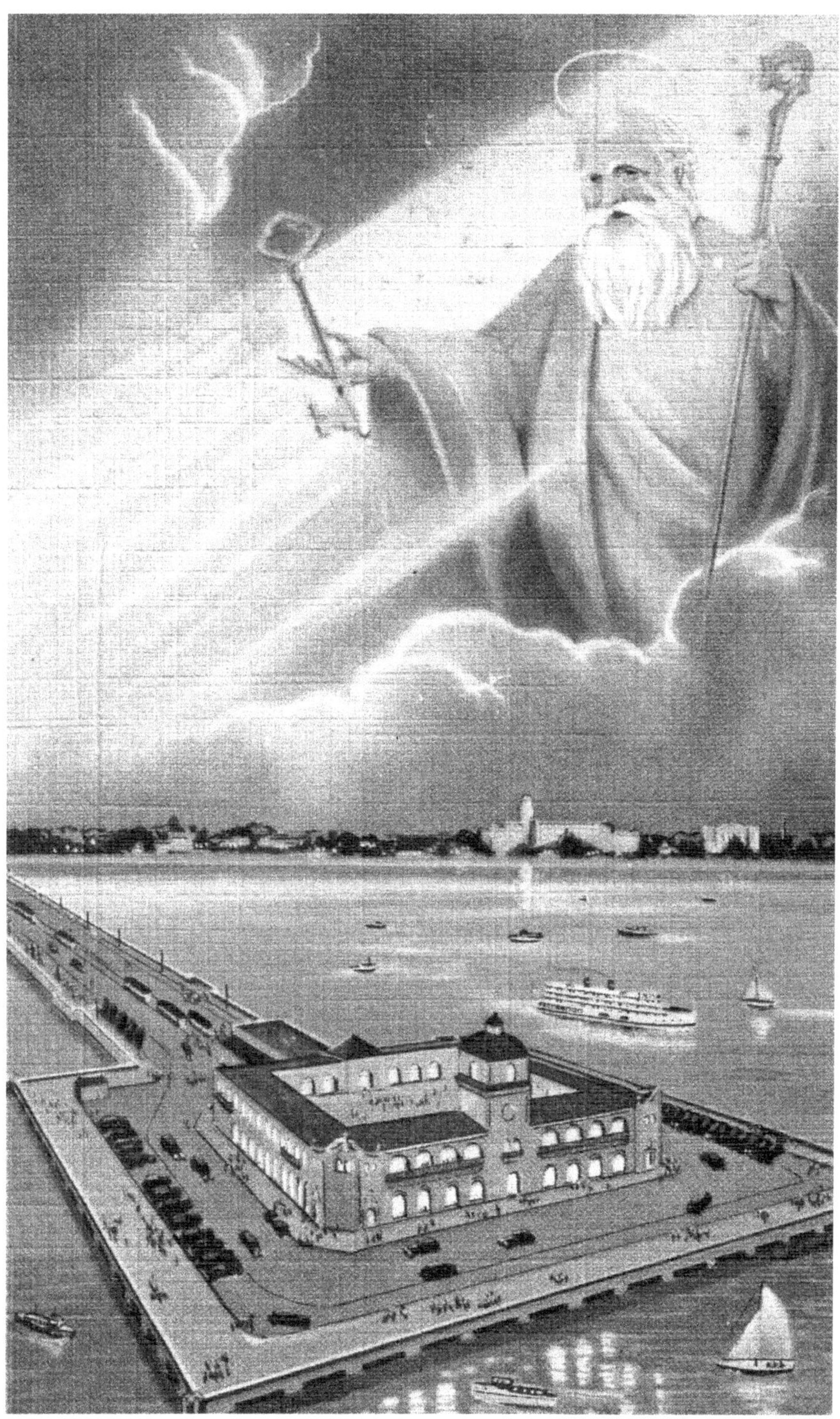

1888 and acquired a building in 1892. In 1891, a second Methodist church, the First Avenue Methodist Church (later Christ Methodist Church), was established. The Baptist church got underway in 1892. In 1895, the First Presbyterian Church was organized.

The first documented clergyman in St. Petersburg was Reverend David Gilkinson Watt, a Congregational minister who arrived in 1885. He was followed a year later by Reverend Gilbert Holt White, an Episcopal clergyman who ministered to the Mission of the Holy Spirit. Reverend White was succeeded by Reverend Henry H. Ten Brock. Reverend G.W. Southwell shepherded the reorganization of the Mission into St. Peter's Church beginning in 1893. He was followed by Reverends F.C. Eldred and T.J. Perdue. Reverend Perdue was succeeded by Reverend Charles McIlvaine Gray. Reverend Gray was "Priest in Charge" from 1902 to 1906 and then became the first rector (1906–11). Reverend Gray was followed by Reverend E.E. Madeira (1911–15).

St. Peter's history in many ways parallels the history of our city as a whole. As the city grew, the church grew, and when hard times came, the church adapted just as the city did. Following World War I, both the city and St. Peter's experienced a boom. Historian Walter Fuller wrote, "It was as if all of war-weary America decided to take a vacation at the same time." So many tourists arrived in St. Pete that local hotels and rooming houses were filled, and "tent cities" had to be set up to accommodate what were known as "tin-can tourists." One of these was set up by the National Guard directly across the street from St. Peter's in Williams Park.

During this postwar boom period, St. Peter's was ministered to by Reverend Wiltshire W. Williams (1915–27). During his tenure, St. Peter's Church was doubled in size to the west and extended to the south, generally achieving its present-day dimensions. The steeple was increased from a two-story to a four-story tower. In 1925, the Abe Pheil family donated chimes for the bell tower. Abe Pheil was an early St. Petersburg mayor and achieved distinction as the world's first airline passenger when he boarded the Benoist Airboat at the St. Petersburg Pier on New Year's Day 1914.

No boom lasts forever, and the post–World War I St. Petersburg boom ended by 1927. The selling and reselling of property in St. Petersburg, at ever increasing prices, was coming to an end. Bank deposits dropped from $46 million in 1925 to $27 million in 1926. By 1931, they were down to $4 million. Population growth also declined. And, of course, tourism declined, especially after the national Great Depression began in 1929.

In 1927, in the early stages of the Depression, Chaplain Evan Alexander Edwards (1927–50) assumed the rectorship of St. Peter's at the age of fifty. He served as rector for twenty-three years. Chaplain Edwards was a veteran of World War I who saw combat and was decorated with the Silver Star. He saw the church through these lean years, even reducing his own salary to help make ends meet. World War II again transformed St. Petersburg and St. Peter's. The tourist economy, which had begun to revive in the late 1930s, again came to a standstill. Fortunately, several city leaders came up with the idea of pitching St. Pete's hotels to the armed forces as a place to house troops while training—training in a place that boasted one of the best climates in the country. In no time, the tourists had been exchanged for some thirty thousand service men and women. Tents were again set up in St. Pete, this time with troops rather than tourists. Chaplain Edwards immediately adapted to this new situation and began to minister to the servicemen boarded in the downtown hotels and adjacent tents. He curtailed pending church renovations, opened the church to the Red Cross and, perhaps most significantly, opened up a "Writing and Recreation Room" for the troops. More than four hundred letters were written home per week by service members or volunteers on their behalf.

After the war, St. Petersburg's and St. Peter's populations again began to boom. In 1949, the church was spending 35 percent of its budget on missionary activities. Support was provided to St. Peter's mother church, St. Bartholomew, which had reverted to mission status in 1941. The Sunday school was expanded, and funds were raised to start a church-sponsored primary school, forerunner of today's Canterbury School. St. Peter's also contributed half the cost of building St. Augustine's African American Episcopal Church. Churches, just like other community institutions, were segregated at this time. After Chaplain Edwards submitted his resignation for the fifth time in 1950, the church finally accepted it.

Chaplain Edwards was followed by Reverend James L. Duncan (1950–61). Reverend Duncan was the great missionary rector of St. Peter's. St. Petersburg was again in a postwar boom period. Consequently, increased membership pressure on St. Peter's facilities and staff was immense, and the potential for additional Episcopal churches in the St. Petersburg area was great. With Father Duncan's leadership, seven new churches were founded between 1952 and 1960. These included St. Thomas, St. Bede's, St. Vincent's, St. Matthew's, St. Giles in Pinellas Park, St. Dunstan's in Largo and Holy Cross. Additionally, Father Duncan laid the groundwork for Suncoast Manor, the Episcopal retirement community (later acquired by the Westminster Communities of Florida). He left St. Peter's in 1961 to become one of three new Diocese of South Florida suffragan bishops, soon assigned to minister to the southeast area. Later, he became bishop of southeast Florida when the Diocese of South Florida was subdivided to create three new dioceses.

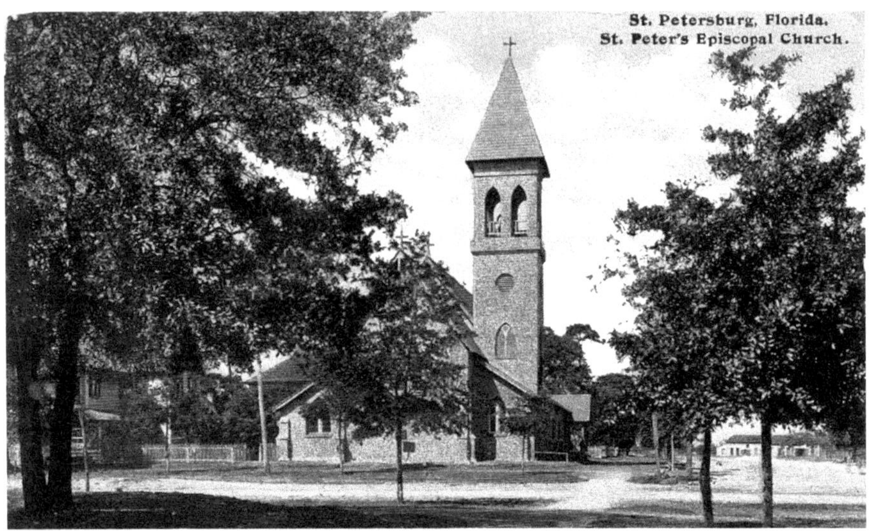

Early postcard view of St. Peter's Cathedral Church, postmarked 1912. The image shows the rectory building at the left, and the streets are unpaved. The postcard is addressed to a clergyman in North Haven, Connecticut, and bears the message, "We obeyed you, The Smiths." Presumably their clergyman told them to be sure to attend church. *Courtesy Michaels Family Collection.*

Reverend Duncan was followed by Reverend LeRoy D. Lawson. Father Lawson led the efforts to establish Peterborough, a low-cost housing facility. He also initiated hospital and social work ministries. After Father Lawson's time, the church continued his social work ministries by operating cold-weather shelters and other outreach programs for the homeless and poor. In 1969, St. Peter's was reborn again as a cathedral along with the creation of the new Diocese of Southwest Florida. Father Lawson now became "dean" of the newly designated cathedral. Next to the diocesan bishop, the senior minister of cathedrals is designated dean. Since 1969, St. Peter's has had six deans. These include the Very Reverend Robert E. Giannini (1981–86), the Very Reverend (later Bishop of the Diocese of Western Missouri) Barry E. Howe (1987–98), the Very Reverend Randall K. Hehr (1998–2002) and the Very Reverend Russell L. Johnson (2004–8). The current dean is the Very Reverend Stephen B. Morris.

In 1990, St. Peter's purchased the adjacent First Baptist Church, including the church's educational building, which was then used by St. Peter's to expand its downtown ministries. In 1994, the cathedral requested the city to designate the First Baptist Church as a local landmark. Many efforts over the years were made to find a use for the First Baptist Church itself. Unfortunately, no party could be found to restore the church and provide an adaptive use. In 2009, St. Peter's formulated a plan in partnership with city preservationists to save at least one part of the church: the towers with the Greek temple–like pillars and stairs facing Williams Park. But the remainder of the church was dismantled to make way for a sanctuary garden and columbarium. The plan was approved by the city, but the garden and columbarium proved not to be feasible. More recently, the remaining First Baptist historic structure and site were purchased by the adjacent Princess Martha Senior Living Community (TJM Properties). The retirement community is itself situated in the former 1920s Neoclassical Princess Martha Hotel, also a city historic landmark.

In 2009, at the cathedral's request, St. Peter's was also designated a local city historic landmark. The decision to landmark St. Peter's was based on both its architectural and historical significance. Architecturally, the cathedral is an excellent example of Florida Late Gothic Revival architecture. Features include its pointed stained-glass windows and doors, steeply pitched intersecting gable roof with projecting eves, verge board (decorative wooden edging), towers with castle-like parapets, lancet windows and vents with tracery, buttresses and interior openwork truss system. St. Peter's is the second-oldest landmarked church in the city. The 10th Street Church of God predates it by one year.

St. Peter's first dean, LeRoy Lawson, once stated, "Every church gives cultural depth to the community. It ought to represent the best in art and use it." Churches are both spiritual and cultural centers. They provide their members with both a spiritual and community identity—a "sense of place," as Eudora Welty called it. This is most reflected in the members themselves—the people. But it is also reflected in the architecture of the church in which they choose to worship, and the best architecture is also art. St. Peter's is rooted in Florida history and in what some call "Real Florida." It is made of the materials of Florida's earth itself, such as heart of pine and north Florida sand brick.

The cathedral has also adapted itself to a changing community: a community of soldiers and sailors in World War II, a church membership needing to grow and expand and fostering services for the homeless and less fortunate in more recent years. Throughout all this, St. Peter's has remained committed to its downtown roots and ministry, and now it may take pride in enjoying the new possibilities of a reawakening downtown.

Sources: Cathedral Church of St. Petersburg, various records; City of St. Petersburg, Development Services Department, "Staff Report: St. Peter's Episcopal Church," CPC Case No.: HPC 09-02; Joseph D. Cushman, *The Sound of Bells: The Episcopal Church in South Florida, 1892–1969* (1976); Walter P. Fuller, *St. Petersburg and Its People* (1972); J. Ira Gore & Son, ed., *Illustrated Edition of the St. Petersburg Times*, September 1899; Karl H. Grismer, *History of St. Petersburg* (1924); Scott Taylor Hartzell, *Remembering St. Petersburg Florida*, vol. 1 (2006); *St. Petersburg Times*, August 21, 1966, June 8, 1963; and Will Michaels, "St. Peter's Cathedral Centennial History" (1989; revised 2009).

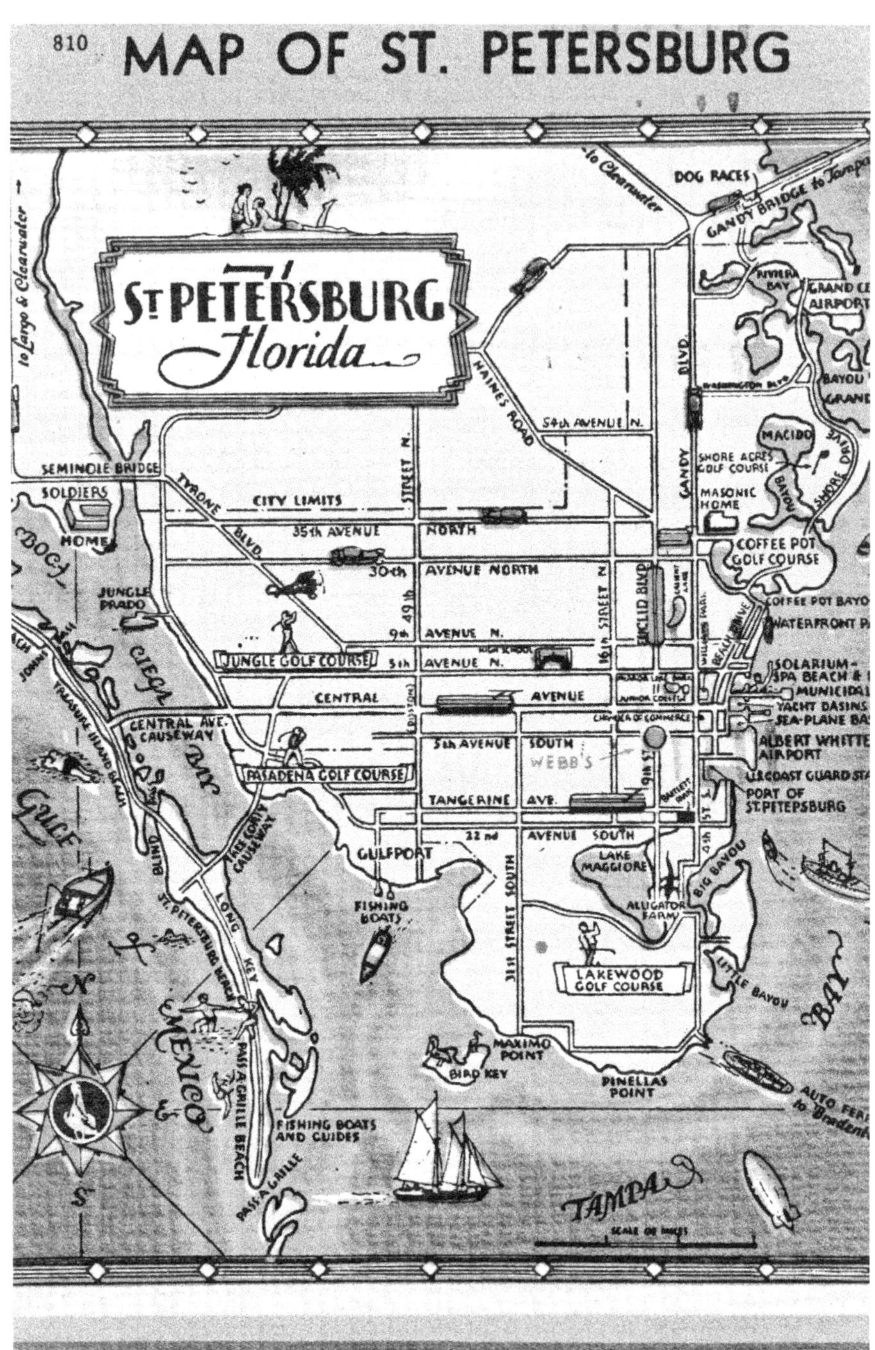

Postcard map of midcentury St. Petersburg prominently displaying the site of Webb's City, image circa 1940. *Courtesy Michaels Family Collection.*

Chapter 5

Doc Webb

Friend of the Little Guy

One of the most colorful characters in St. Petersburg's history was James Earl "Doc" Webb. Historian Raymond Arsenault called him a "marketing wizard of the first order" and a "self-made man who turned his life into a rags-to-riches success story worthy of Horatio Alger."

Webb was born in Nashville, Tennessee, in 1899. He was forced to drop out of school at the age of nine after his father was seriously injured in an accident. As a youth, he set pins in a bowling alley and peddled milk and vegetables on the street. But his ultimate calling was that of a "medicine man." At the age of twenty, he reinvented himself as "Doc" Webb, purveyor of patent medicines and magical herbs. His most profitable patent medicine was known as "Doc Webb's 608," a cure for venereal disease. It cost forty-five cents to make and sold for five dollars. Reportedly, it worked pretty well. Doc Webb was, in fact, a registered pharmacist. But unlike his contemporary, C. Perry Snell, he was unschooled. He became manager and part owner of Economy Drugs in Knoxville.

In 1925, like so many of St. Pete's early transplants, Webb found it necessary to move to a warmer climate because of his health. He was offered a partnership with Hayworth Johnson, an old friend who had recently opened a small drugstore with a mere three hundred square feet of merchandising space on the northern fringe of one of St. Petersburg's African American neighborhoods.

Webb arrived in St. Pete at just the wrong time. The boom that the city was experiencing was about ready to collapse. Nevertheless, he bought out

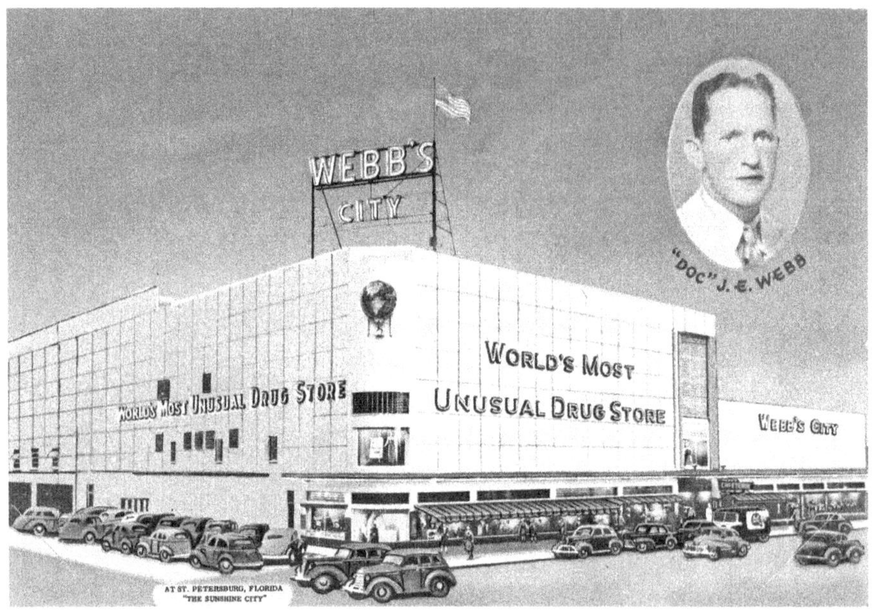

Doc Webb and his signature Webb's City main building, part of a seventy-seven-store complex covering approximately seven blocks, image circa 1945. *Courtesy Michaels Family Collection.*

his partner. He changed the name of the drugstore to Webb's Cut Rate Drug Company—a sign of things to come. Throughout the 1920s, he cultivated bargain-basement price hunters, and this fortuitously positioned him nicely to take advantage of the Depression of the 1930s, when nearly everyone was hunting bargains.

LITTLE GUY'S FRIEND

He promised to undersell his competitors by at least 10 percent on every item. Needless to say, this did not make him popular with the chamber of commerce. In fact, young ladies from "proper families" were forbidden by their parents from shopping at Webb's. But chamber schmoozing was not his goal. He promoted himself as "the little man's friend," not the friend of the well-to-do. At a time when most businesses were cutting back, Webb's Cut Rate Drug Company expanded. No longer limiting his fare to drugs, he expanded into groceries, meats, clothing, cigarettes, photography, electrical supplies and household appliances, fishing tackle, luggage, coffee shops and a floral shop. Webb's City additionally had its own nurse to provide first aid to its customers. Webb's famous basement cafeteria began by selling a full breakfast for two cents. This attracted hundreds of customers to what at the time was a kind of out-of-the-way location for breakfast. Of course, after the cafeteria became established, the price was raised to fourteen cents. Wednesday was "chicken day." Webb sold chickens, two to a bag for seventeen to nineteen cents per pound. Sometimes the lines would be a block long on that day. Other promotions included "Topsy-turvy Day," when you might buy cigars at the meat counter and underwear in produce, or "Dollar Day," when dollar bills would be sold for ninety-nine cents!

Successful Showman

Webb was not only a successful businessman but also a successful showman. As Arsenault wrote, "Vaudeville and circus acts, dancing chickens, talking mermaids, scantily clad bathing beauties known as 'Poster Girls,' oversized floats in the Festival of States parade—no advertising gimmick was too bizarre or too outrageous for Doc Webb, the master showman of volume sales." His Poster Girls traveled all over the country and even abroad, advertising Webb's City and sunny St. Petersburg. Anyone who is a St. Petersburg "old-timer" has some memory of Webb's City. The author bought his first Christmas tree at Webb's in about 1974. He also has fond memories of his uncle, who would come down to St. Pete from "up north" for yearly visits. One of Uncle Al's favorite St. Pete attractions was Webb's. Even in the 1970s, Webb's still featured dancing chickens, mermaid shows and, of course, all the bargains.

Historian Walter Fuller described Webb's City as "the biggest, certainly the noisiest pioneer 'shopping center' in the country…carried on like a perpetual merchandising hurricane." Doc Webb was one of Fuller's favorite local persons. Webb contributed to one of Fuller's runs for local elected office, and being the smart businessperson he was, he contributed to Fuller's opponent as well. But Webb and Fuller did not always see eye to eye. In the 1950s, Webb sought to prevent development at Central Plaza, which was known at the time as Goose Pond because of the flooding that occurred there in a heavy rain. He wanted the area chopped into smaller parcels, making it more difficult to have a large development. Fuller was then chair of the Planning and Zoning Board and successfully opposed Webb's attempt to prevent the Central Plaza project.

Astute Businessman

Webb accepted IOUs and extended credit to nearly everyone. His goal was volume, and in order to achieve this, he was willing to risk some bad debts. "I didn't care a damn about money, I wanted customers," he said. In 1940, he sought to expand his business but had difficulty raising capital. He qualified as a securities underwriter and offered $200,000 of stock in Webb's City at 7 percent interest. He announced the availability of the stock in a two-page ad. His customers came by the droves and bought up all the stock in a mere thirty hours. By buying into the business, the public was stating that this was their store, too.

By the mid-1930s, Doc Webb had turned a tiny drugstore into the "World's Most Unusual Drug Store," a seventy-seven-store complex covering seven or eight city blocks. It was a forerunner of the post–World War II shopping center. Tyrone Gardens at 9th Avenue and Tyrone Boulevard North did not come along until the early 1950s, to be followed by Central Plaza in 1952. Only Walter Fuller's 1920s Jungle Prado shopping center, the first in the county and one of the first in the nation, predated Webb's. By 1936, his sales topped $1 million per year. By 1941, they were $4 million. Webb prided himself on offering only nationally advertised brands of merchandise, not off-brands. By 1973, Webb's City had more than 1,500 employees and attracted 60,000 shoppers daily. Nowadays, a trip down Interstate 75 and other major thoroughfares hype Disney World. Go back in time before Disney, and those same billboard locations hyped "Webb's City—The World's Most Unusual Drug Store."

Fuller described buying butter at Webb's during World War II. Butter was then rationed, a scare commodity, and highly priced. But Fuller decided to treat himself even though the cost of a pound of butter was more than seventy cents. Just as he put the butter in his shopping cart, Webb's across-the-street competitor put up a sign advertising butter below seventy cents. Fuller said that Webb then became a whirlwind of action. He reduced the cost of his butter to fifty-nine cents. The competitor again reduced his price, and then so did Webb again. By the time Fuller checked out, the price of his butter was down to nineteen cents. But by the time he loaded his groceries into his car, the price had gone back up to seventy-four cents.

Doc Webb was a free spirit. He did things his own way, without much regard to what others thought. In 1938, he challenged the Bristol-Myers Company. He refused to sell Ipana toothpaste at the manufacturer's recommended retail price. He wanted to discount it. Bristol-Myers sued Webb, taking the case all the way to the Florida Supreme Court. Ultimately, Webb prevailed, adding further to what Arsenault called his "populist mystique." In Webb's opinion, competition was the "soul of business—and life."

CIVIL RIGHTS ERA

While African Americans could shop at Webb's City, they could not eat at the lunch counters. In 1960, thirty African American Gibbs Junior College students staged demonstrations at Webb's and the S.H. Kress store. Both stores had lunch counters. They were refused entry and left quietly. Reverend

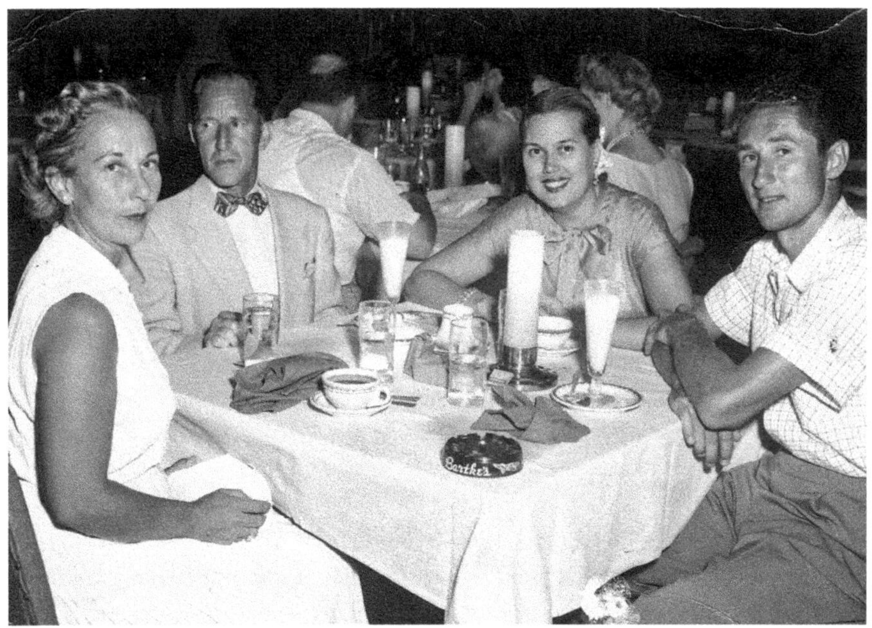

Doc Webb (with bow tie) and his wife, Arretta (left), dine with St. Petersburg tennis champion and coach Dan Sullivan and his wife, Casey. Webb was an avid tennis player, image circa 1955. *Courtesy Shirley O'Sullivan.*

Ted Lockhart, later president of the Carter G. Woodson African American Museum, was a student at Gibbs College and a member of the NAACP Youth Council at the time. He remembered participating in the picketing, much to his grandmother's displeasure. African Americans led by Dr. Ralph Wimbish boycotted Webb's for nine months. In terms of race relations, like most people of his generation, Webb was a product of his times. Lunch counters were finally integrated throughout the city in 1961. In 2000, a very successful local musical was produced called *Webb's City: The Musical*. It was written and directed by Bill Leavengood with lyrics and music composed by Lee Ahlin. Leavengood said at the time that Webb's portrayal embraced the merchant's concern for people who had to struggle, including the African Americans who were among his steady customers. "He was heroic. If he had a fault, he was monomaniacal in the pursuit of his business."

WEBB'S CLOSES

Webb was married in 1934 to Arretta Brooks, a native of his home city of Knoxville. He had two children, Eleanor and James Earl Webb Jr. His son flew in the Ninth Air Force during World War II and was shot down on D-Day but survived with only minor injuries. Doc Webb was an avid tennis player and at one time was president of the St. Petersburg Tennis Club. He also loved fast cars and speedboats. He was a member of First Baptist Church at Williams Park, as well as a member of many local civic associations.

Webb sold his business just prior to the decline of downtown St. Pete in the late 1970s, caused in part by newer commercial developments at Tyrone Square Mall and Central Plaza. Webb's City closed its doors for good in 1978. It is little known that Doc Webb was once interviewed by famed World War II war correspondent Ernie Pyle. Pyle was known as the GI's reporter. He wrote about the troops in the trenches, not so much the generals. Perhaps he saw a kindred soul in Doc Webb, champion of the little guy. Pyle wrote of Webb, "He talks 'country' Tennessee talk and is as nervous as a witch. He is flexed, foxed, strained for the leap. He is as sharp as the serpent's tooth.... Doc Webb was born nervous and keyed up. An uncanny lightning strikes within him a million times a day. All the time he keeps winding up, like an airplane motor in a dive."

Sources: Raymond Arsenault, *St. Petersburg and the Florida Dream: 1888–1950* (1988/1996); Rick Baker, *Mangroves to Major League: A Timeline of St. Petersburg, Florida* (2000); Walter P. Fuller, *St. Petersburg and Its People* (1972); Karl H. Grismer, *History of St. Petersburg* (1924); Hampton Dunn, *Yesterday's St. Petersburg* (1973); *St. Petersburg Times*, various dates; Webb's City, "Facts and History"; and a conversation with Reverend Ted Lockhart.

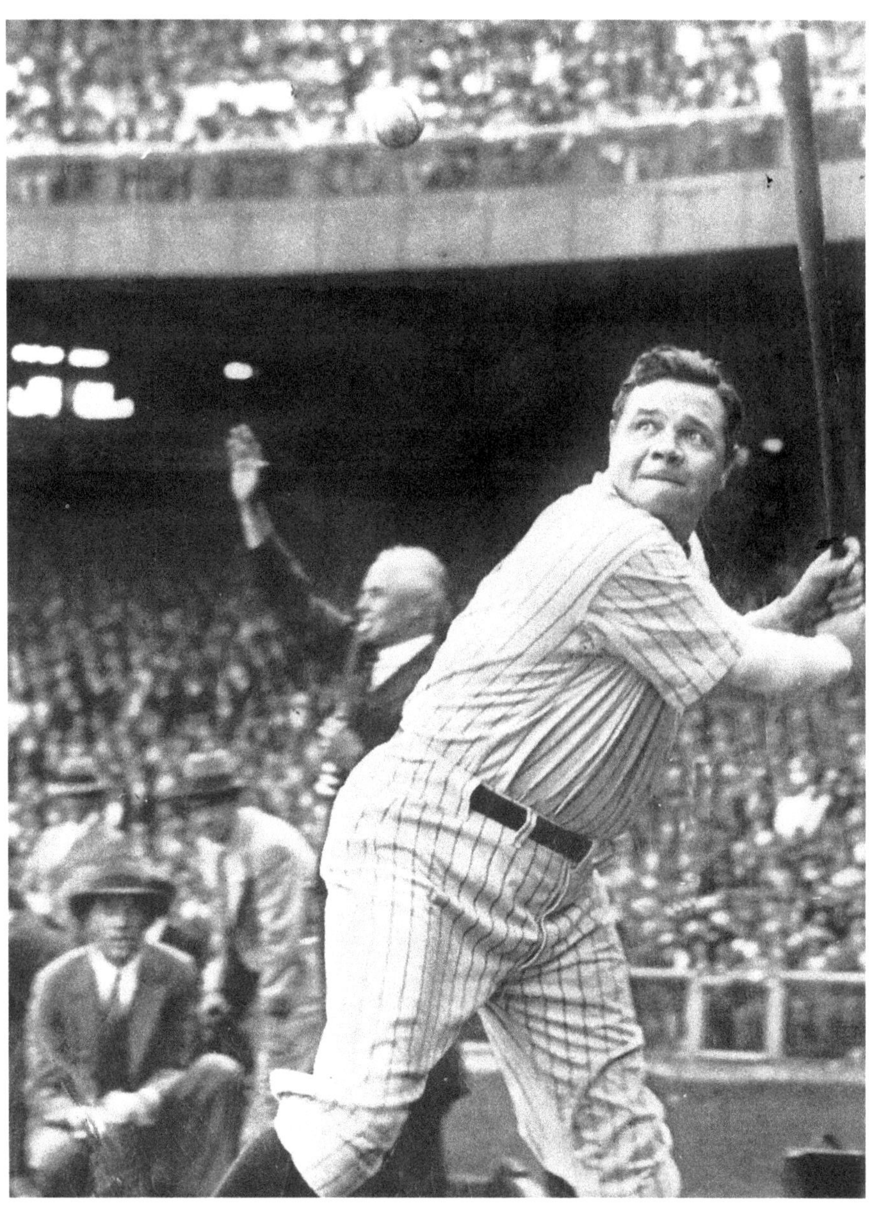

Babe Ruth, who batted left, was the first player to hit sixty home runs in one season (1927). *Courtesy Julia Ruth Stevens.*

Chapter 6

Babe Ruth's Longest Home Run

Major League Spring Training began in St. Petersburg on February 27, 1914, with the St. Louis Browns (now the Orioles). While the Browns were here only one year, St. Petersburg was host to eight other major-league teams over the next one hundred years. Among these teams was the New York Yankees, who held spring training in St. Pete for thirty years beginning in 1925 and ending in 1961, with a few gaps in between. That team included Babe Ruth, generally regarded as the greatest player ever.

Ruth first came to St. Pete with the Yankees in 1925 and continued with them until 1934, returning to St. Pete the following year for an encore as a member of the Boston Braves. George Herman "Babe" Ruth Jr., nicknamed "the Bambino" and "the Sultan of Swat," was known for his hitting brilliance, setting career records in his time for home runs, slugging, RBIs and bases on balls. He helped the Yankees win seven pennants and four World Series titles. Ruth, who batted left, was the first player to hit sixty home runs in one season (1927). This mark was not surpassed until another Yankee right fielder, Roger Maris, hit sixty-one in 1961. (Maris had the advantage of a season with ten more games and fifty more at-bats.) Ruth was a great pitcher as well as slugger, and some of his pitching records still hold to this day.

In 1919, Ruth was a member of the Boston Red Sox when they held spring training in Tampa. Ruth may have made his first excursion to St. Pete at the time, but no record of that has been found. During the 1919 spring training season, while playing against the New York Giants in Tampa, Ruth hit a home run. For years this was considered Ruth's longest home run and was probably longer than any other hit by a player during Ruth's time. The feat is commemorated on a plaque near Tampa's Plant Field at the University of Tampa. Baseball historian Bill Jenkinson believes that Ruth's hit traveled 552 feet in the air. While the home run's exact distance may be debatable, it was definitely impressive. Giants' manager John McGraw stated at the time, "I believe it's the longest hit I ever saw." Coincidentally, St. Petersburg mayor Al Lang was in Tampa to lobby the Giants to relocate to St. Petersburg for future spring trainings when Ruth hit his impressive homer. This inspired the mayor to push to get Ruth and the Yankees, rather than the Giants, to come to St. Pete.

For many years, there has been speculation that Ruth hit an even longer homer in St. Pete from Waterfront Park, which was a little north of today's Al Lang Stadium, to the old West Coast Inn, approximately on the site of today's Hilton Hotel. But documentation for this was lacking. Recent research has better confirmed this claim. Ruth appears to have hit a ball to the West Coast Inn during batting practice in 1925. But the question is, did he also do this in an exhibition major-league game? Historian Bill Jenkinson has identified fifteen home runs hit by Ruth over the course of his career during major-league exhibition games at Waterfront Park, and he identifies only seven of these as having any chance of landing near the West Coast Inn. An actual recorded reference to the West Coast Inn has been found in only two of these games, one in 1933 and one in 1934. The 1933 home run was reported as "bounding almost to the West Coast Inn." But the best candidate for Ruth's record-breaking hit occurred in 1934.

In 1934, Ruth was coming to the end of his career. That year was his last with the Yankees. His salary was down from a high of $80,000 in 1930 to $35,000. He still could bat and hit home runs with exceptional frequency, but his running and fielding had badly deteriorated. He would continue in baseball one additional year as a member of the Boston Braves. His last year with the Yankees did not start out well. Prior to annual spring training in St. Pete, he came down with the flu and lost sixteen pounds. He usually arrived in St. Pete in January to enjoy the warm weather and recreation prior to beginning training in March. But because of the flu, he had to delay his departure and also his annual birthday party at the Jungle Country Club Hotel on Park Street, now Admiral Farragut Academy. Celebrating his fortieth birthday in New York, he received a mammoth golf bag from his wife, Claire, and his daughters, Julia and Dorothy. He finally reached St. Pete on February 9, and fifteen minutes after arriving at the Jungle Hotel, he was on the links. A day later, he hit a massive 250-yard drive with an iron (not a driver), followed by a second 220-yard shot, and scored the first-ever double eagle at the Jungle Club's seventeenth hole. Ruth said that he played golf to keep his weight down, as well as for enjoyment. "I am depending on golf to help me regain my top-notch physical condition." At a delayed birthday party given to him by city publicity agent John Lodwick, Ruth said, "They have been saying that this would be my last year as an active player in the big leagues, but I'm not certain about that. Since I came south, I have been feeling fine and my legs feel strong. Whether I play after this year depends on the success I have this season."

Once spring training started, Ruth made some changes in his routine. He used a thirty-eight-ounce bat—lighter than usual. He changed his grip a little, maybe a cue from golf. He was feeling better, fully recovered from the flu. And it began to show. The Yankees were practicing at Miller Huggins Field at Crescent Lake. "Babe Fools Experts by Fast Start," read the subtitle of an article in the St. Petersburg *Evening Independent* by Jeff Moshier. "Ruth is up to his old tricks—hitting home runs at a record-breaking clip, and confounding not only the experts but probably himself....Today, at 40, the Babe admits himself that he is all but through. He hopes to play in 100 games for the Yankees this season but finally agrees with the boys that his days as a player are numbered....In the face of all this Ruth is enjoying probably the greatest spring of his 20 year career in the majors. He has cracked out six home runs in seven games, driving in 16 runs and scored 10. His batting average is .390, a mark he hasn't scored since 1923."

Ruth himself at first attributed his energetic spring start to a new type of ball. A 1934 *New York Times* article quoted Ruth saying, "Boy when you hit that new ball we're going to play with this year it sure does take a ride. I've just been hitting them high and far, like no other ball I've ever swung at. You certainly can send it on a long journey." The article went on to say that "the Bambino was referring to some terrific drives which cracked off his bat, mostly to the far right field, among the pines fringing Crescent Lake." But as it turns out there was really not a new ball. The Yankees were in the American League, and the National League adopted the American League ball that Ruth had been playing with all along in 1934. There were only slight differences between the two balls anyway. A major change in ball composition had not been made since 1931. This change resulted in an average reduction in scores and home runs per game and, logically, shorter home runs.

Moshier continued to write:

> *Usually Ruth starts slowly in the spring and has found it difficult to find the right field range with any degree of consistency in the exhibition games.... His home runs at Waterfront Park in the ten years of training here can be counted on two hands. The Babe's start this spring is great encouragement for the Yankees, whose pennant hopes may rest on his aging shoulders. If he is able to play 100 games and push his batting average well above the .300 mark, with 30 or more home runs tossed in for good measure, the Yankees will make it hot for the rest of the league and may confound the experts by battling right down to the wire for the pennant. Always a great showman and the one to do the unexpected, Ruth evidently is intent on closing out his major league career in a blaze of glory if his showing this spring is an indication of what to expect from him this summer.*

Ruth finished the spring season with a .429 batting average with hits hard and long. He led the team in runs batted in (RBIs). The Yankees really did "make it hot" for the rest of the league in the regular season, finishing in second place, but seven games back of the Tigers. While Ruth's batting average dropped to .288, he hit twenty-two home runs, second behind fellow team mate Lou Gehrig with forty-nine. (Gehrig received the Triple Crown for leading the league in batting average, home runs and runs batted in.)

On March 17, 1934, the *Times* reported that Ruth "hit a whistling line drive over the canvas screen in the right field for the first homer of the season....The King, who is playing spring baseball with a much more serious mein [*sic*] than in other years, appeared determined to smack one of [pitcher] Bob Smith's offerings out of the park." While this was described as "one of Ruth's hardest hit spring homers," there was no mention of the West Coast Inn.

However, it was eight days later, on March 25, 1934, that Ruth appeared to hit his long-neglected record-breaking home run at Waterfront Park. The best account of the event found to date comes from the *Boston Herald* and was written by Burt Whitman under the partial headline "Ruth Lashes Out 6th Circuit Clout." It was an exhibition game between the Yankees and the Boston Braves. The weather was hot—ninety degrees in the shade. Ruth's first threat was in the third inning when he hit one of his famous high-altitude balls. "The Bambino lashed a pitch off Huck Betts so high into the air that you'd excuse the Rabbit [the Boston shortstop's nickname, along with the "Springfield Kid"] for getting a stiff neck and missing the catch. For him, to scamper backwards, head up and straight back and then catch this towering drive was a miracle, when you recall the way he catches them at his

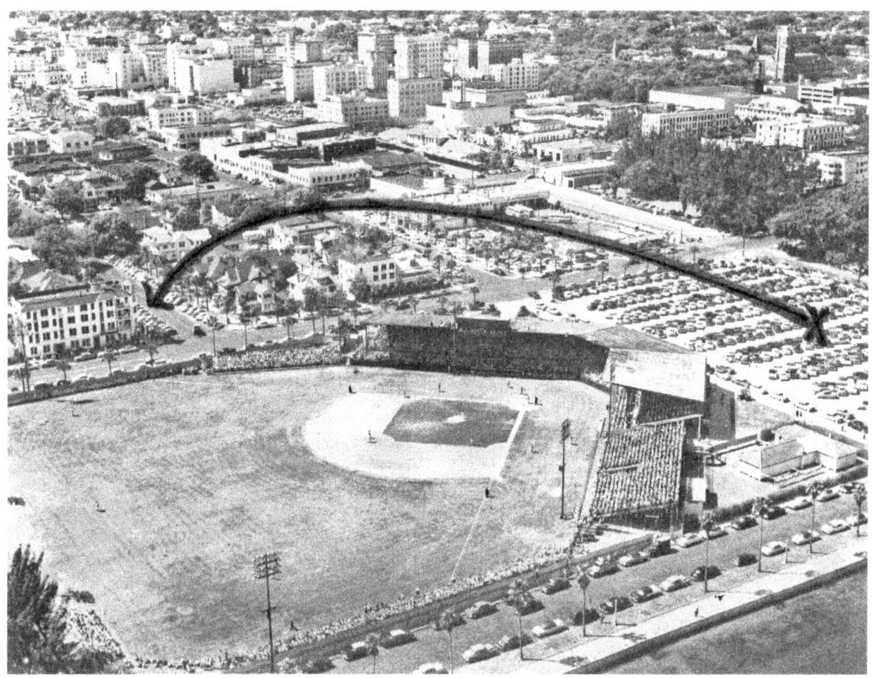

Ruth hit a 624-foot home run from the Waterfront Park Stadium to the West Coast Inn at the southwest corner of 1st Street and 3rd Avenue South, the site of today's Hilton Hotel. This photo shows the general trajectory. Waterfront Park's home plate was near the center of the Al Lang parking lot. Photo is of the first Al Lang Stadium, image 1950. *Courtesy St. Petersburg Museum of History.*

belt line. You'd hardly be surprised to see the force of that falling ball, like a meteor, bury the Springfield kid several yards in the Florida sand."

But Ruth was back again in the fifth inning. Whitman continued, "The crowd of 1200 got the customary home run treat from Babe Ruth. He socked a Betts pitch 10,000 leagues to right field…far over the canvas and almost into the West Coast Inn [southwest corner of 3rd Avenue and 1st Street], where the Braves live between games. It was George's sixth of the season." *St. Pete Times* sports writer Pete Norris, under the headline "Ruth's Blast Over Right Field Fence Gives Sunday Crowd A Thrill," recorded that "Babe Ruth tied the score in the fifth when he hit one of his longest home runs over the right field fence." Beyond these accounts, the details get fuzzy. Some old-timers are quoted in the press years later as seeing a ball bounce on the front porch of the hotel. One said it was the second balcony of the hotel. "[Ruth] once hit a ball onto the second balcony of the West Coast Inn. Must have traveled 500 feet. Man, how it shook up the people sitting on the porch." Unfortunately, none of these recollections can be tied to a specific game date.

The "500 feet" recollection would have been an understatement. While it is debatable whether the ball hit short of the hotel and then rolled to it, took a bounce in front of the hotel up to the balcony or actually hit a balcony directly, it has been established that the ball traveled a measured 624 feet plus some inches. The distance, measuring from the old home plate location at Waterfront Park to the closest part of the now demolished West Coast Inn, was surveyed and verified by the George F. Young civil engineering company in 2008. Many previous home run records in Major League Baseball have been reassessed recently. According to Tim Reid of the Committee to Commemorate Babe Ruth, the West Coast Inn home run is now believed to be perhaps the longest hit ever off major-league pitching. Reid, an engineer, estimated the actual distance in the air as no less than 610 feet. Bill Jenkinson, baseball historian and author of *Baseball's Ultimate Power: Ranking the All-Time Great Distance Home Run Hitters* (2010), stated in a communication to the author, "Babe Ruth's 'West Coast Inn Home Run' on March 25 1934 likely ranks as the longest drive ever hit against Major League pitching. It flew far beyond 500 feet, and may have reached the forbidden distance of 600 feet. For many years, I have steadfastly believed that no human being could hit a baseball 600 feet, but, based upon new research on this blow, I admit I was probably mistaken."

No record has been found of Ruth himself commenting on the homer at the time it was hit. But when Ruth was sick with oral cancer and making a last hurrah tour in 1948, he returned to the site of St. Pete's downtown Waterfront Park Stadium. Asked what his greatest accomplishment there was, he replied, "The day I hit the…ball against that…hotel!" He did not say "near" the hotel but "against" the hotel. In 1935, Ruth joined the Boston Braves. Maybe at least a part of the decision-making that went into bringing Ruth on at the age of forty-one, aside from his world-famous reputation, was the West Coast Inn homer.

Jenkinson also wrote regarding Ruth, "Not only did he set distance records in every major league ballpark (including National League stadiums where he played only infrequently), he also set similar standards in hundreds of other fields, where he made exhibition and barnstorming appearances. Amazingly, many of those records remain unequaled, which is to say that Ruth is a true athletic anachronism. In virtually every other field of endeavor in which physical performance can be measured, there are no Ruthian equivalents. In 1921 alone, which was Ruth's best tape measure season, he hit at least one 500 foot home run in all eight American League cities."

St. Petersburg *Evening Independent* journalist Jeff Moshier also was impressed with Ruth's West Coast Inn homer. He wrote, "Yesterday, as the Yanks went down in their first defeat of the training season before the Boston Braves, he [Ruth] hit a towering drive that cleared the right field barrier well into fair territory with plenty of room to spare." Then Moshier went on to comment as an aside that "his home run smashes over the flag pole on the center field fence about eight or nine years ago has never been approached." Material for yet another Ruth story!

Sources: *Boston Globe*, various dates; *Brooklyn Daily Eagle*, various dates; *Eugene Register-Guard*, various dates; *Evening Independent*, various dates; Charles Fountain, *Under the March Sun: The Story of Spring Training* (2009); *Hartfort Courant*, various dates; William J. Jenkinson, "Long Distance Home Runs," *Baseball Almanac* (1986), and *Baseball's Ultimate Power: Ranking the All-Time Great Distance Home Run Hitters* (2010); Kevin M. McCarthy, *Babe Ruth in Florida* (2002); *New York Times*, various dates; *St. Petersburg Times*, various dates; *Boston Herald*, various dates; *Sporting News*, various dates; Will Michaels, *The Making of St. Petersburg* (2012); *Sarasota Journal*, various dates; and communications with Tim Reid and Bill Jenkinson.

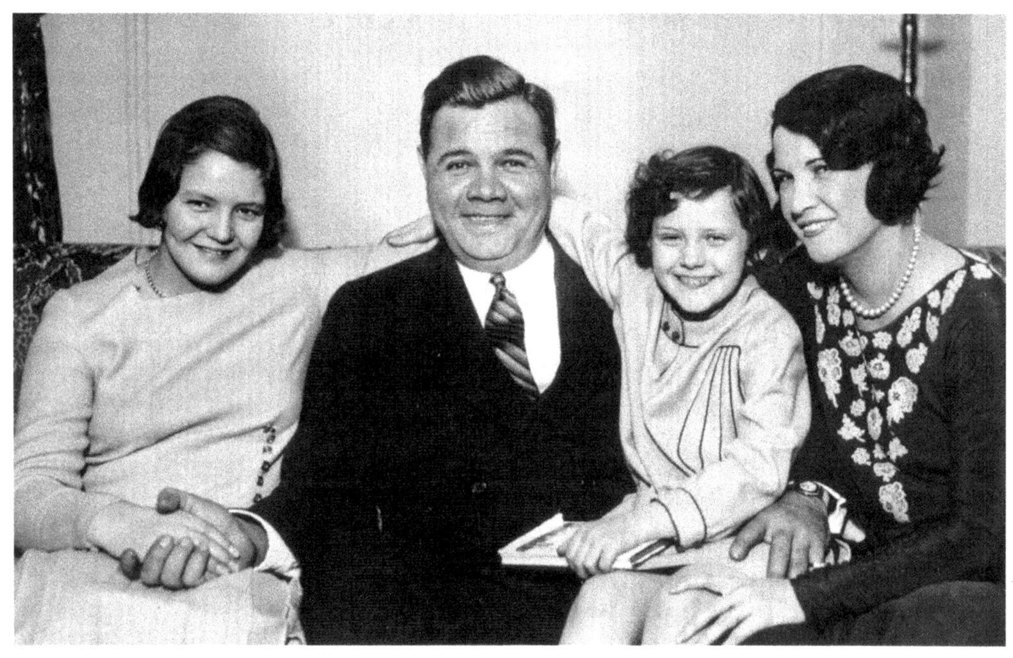

The Ruth family. *Left to right*: Julia, the Babe, Dorothy and Claire, image circa 1930. *Courtesy Julia Ruth Stevens.*

Chapter 7

Conversation with Babe Ruth's Daughter

Babe Ruth's first wife, Helen Woodford, died in an accident. Ruth subsequently married actress and model Claire Merritt Hodgson in 1929 and adopted her daughter, Julia. In 2013, the author had the privilege of interviewing Julia, and this chapter is based on that interview. At that time, Julia was ninety-seven years old and had not been in St. Petersburg since 1943. Her married name is Julia Ruth Stevens.

The Ruth family often rented homes in St. Pete during the spring training season, frequently in the Old Northeast area and Snell Isle. Julia was twelve at the time Babe and Claire married. Claire had married her first husband as a young teenager. She was sixteen when Julia was born. "Mother was only sixteen years older than I was. She married very young. So I went along on lots of trips that normally I wouldn't have done if I was younger. We were almost like sisters."

Asked what it was like to be in St. Pete with a dad who was the most famous baseball player in the world, Julia replied:

> *Just like anywhere else. When I met people, if it was away from home, I never told anybody who I was…I wanted people to like me for myself, not because I was Babe Ruth's daughter.*
>
> *When I mentioned St. Pete to my New York friends, they said, "That's the old folk's home." I said it is not. There are some elderly people there, but there are plenty of young people also. I went to school at the Aiken Open Air School…I loved St. Pete. The place that we were renting was nearby so I could walk* [to school].

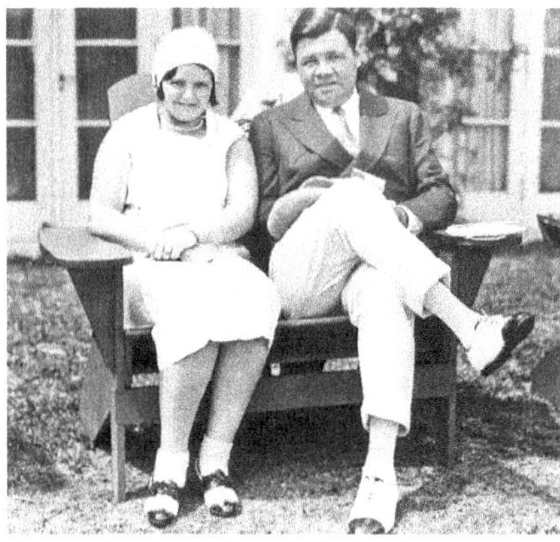

Julia Ruth and the Babe, image circa 1930. *Courtesy Julia Ruth Stevens.*

This may have been the Flori-de-Leon on 4th Avenue North or a nearby private residence. Julia does remember living in a "penthouse" one year, probably the Flori. Babe Ruth and Lou Gehrig rented penthouses there in 1933. The Open Air School was located in downtown St. Petersburg where Presbyterian Towers is now located, 430 Bay Street Northeast. The school was the first private school in the city, dating from 1912.

She noted that during the Depression years of the 1930s, "money was very tight" and lots of people rented their homes out. "Most of the time, mother and Daddy rented a place and mother would bring a cook, and Daddy would not have to eat in restaurants and eat the wrong food. Mother was very particular about what he ate. She wanted him to eat a healthy diet. I think it contributed a great deal to his longevity [as a ballplayer]."

"Mother and Daddy were good friends of Billy DeBeck and his family." DeBeck was an internationally syndicated cartoonist who drew *Barney Google and Snuffy Smith*. He maintained a seasonal home on Snell Isle. In fact, St. Petersburg boasted a small group of nationally known cartoonists for many years. In addition to DeBeck, there were Wally Bishop, who drew *Muggs and Skeeter*, and Pop Momand, who created *Keeping Up with the Joneses*.

> *I met my best friend forever, Pinky Parker, at Mrs. Aiken's Open Air School. She used to come up* [to New Hampshire] *and visit us every summer because St. Pete got so hot. There didn't used to be that many air conditioned places.*
>
> *There was no license required to drive, and my friend Pinky was only fourteen years old and she was driving all over the city. My father* [Babe] *was absolutely floored by this. I told him you have nothing to worry about; she is a very good driver. I was not permitted to get a license in New York City until I was twenty-one years old. If I had an accident when I was under age, the people* [affected] *would jump on him and sue him.*
>
> *We liked to play cards, and also there was a place…where they would have out-of-town bands come like Duke Ellington. There was a little bit of a flurry about Duke Ellington because this was back in the 1930s, and he*

> *was colored. He had a wonderful orchestra and that blew over. After that, there wasn't any kind of problem.*
>
> *I loved St. Petersburg. I really did. And Pinky was not the only friend because she had friends, and we would all get together. Sometimes there would be four of us, and we would play cards. We just had a wonderful, wonderful time, and I loved St. Petersburg.*

A favorite place Julia remembered was the Jungle Country Club Hotel, now Admiral Farragut Academy on Park Street near Boca Ciega Bay. The Jungle Hotel was built by Walter P. Fuller and designed by architect Henry Taylor in 1925. Taylor also designed the Vinoy and St. Mary's Church. "The Jungle Hotel was beautiful. It had a wonderful dance floor. They used to have an orchestra there every Saturday night. There was always dancing. I really loved the Jungle Hotel. There was a streetcar that ran almost there [from downtown], and I could take the streetcar to visit my girlfriend and go to the movies and things like that. Lots of times we would go to the beach and go swimming." She also remembered going to the Million Dollar Pier for frosted root beer.

> *The Jungle had a beautiful golf course. Daddy bought me a set of clubs, and I tried but I wasn't very good. I could generally drive the ball, but once it landed in the sand trap…I tried so hard to get it out my caddie was laughing. "You took sixty-three strokes to get it out!"*
>
> *Daddy loved both golfing and fishing. That's the reason he always went down* [to St. Pete] *in January when he could do these things. Once the* [baseball spring training] *season began, which was in March, he did not have as much time to do that. It* [also] *gave him a chance to get out of the cold weather in New York. It was great.*
>
> *Mother and I most of the time would go to the exhibit games. I didn't go to every game. Mother did. And lots of the time she would go with June Gomez, the wife of Lefty Gomez. Lefty was a tryout from California, a rookie, but was a terrific pitcher.* [Lefty played for the Yankees from 1930 to 1942. He was a five-time World Series champion. His wife had a brief career on Broadway before they were married.]
>
> *Once in a while, I would go to the baseball games where the players were all seventy-five years old. They were called the Kids and Kubs.* [The Kids and Cubs softball team began in 1930. It continues to this day. Signature uniforms are white and red with bow ties.] *I loved St. Pete. It was such a friendly town.*

In the 1932 World Series, Babe hit his controversial "called shot" at Wrigley Field in Chicago. He made a pointing gesture that many interpreted as being in the direction of the bleachers in center field. With a two-strike count, he then proceeded to hit a home run to that very spot. "Mother was at the 'called shot' game. Believe it or not, so was Cardinal Spellman of New York. And he said absolutely he did point regardless of what Charlie Root the pitcher said. Several reporters asked Daddy how would you have felt after you did that if you hadn't hit a home run, and Daddy said, 'Pretty foolish, I'm afraid.'" Francis Spellman was auxiliary bishop of Boston at the time. Others in the stands included Franklin Delano Roosevelt, then a candidate for president; his son, James Roosevelt; and a very young John Paul Stevens, later to become Supreme Court justice.

> *One time, Mark Roth who was the traveling secretary of the New York Yankees, was walking up and down in the dugout and ringing his hands and brushing his hair back, and Daddy said, "What's the matter?" The game was tied, and he said if we don't catch the train* [to the next game] *we are going to have to stay over. Daddy said, "Oh, is that all." It was the ninth inning. Daddy got up and hit a home run, the game was over and they caught the train.*
>
> *Daddy certainly could hit a long ball and a pretty high one too. I think he was the best ball player we ever had...He also had such a genuine love for people. He loved his fans, even if they booed him. (He struck out a lot.) He said they're the ones who pay my salary, and I love all my fans.* [Daddy] *was a very, very generous man, and he did absolutely love children. I couldn't have had a better father.*

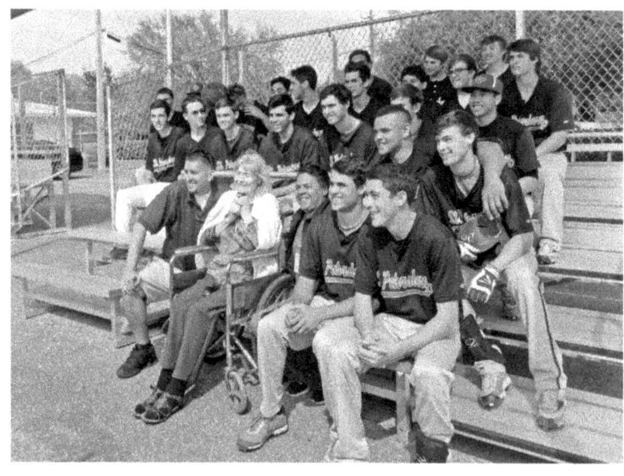

Julia Ruth Stevens, Babe Ruth's daughter, at Huggins-Stengel Field (Crescent Lake Baseball Park), where the Yankees and Babe Ruth practiced. The author had the honor of escorting Julia on a tour of sites associated with Babe Ruth in St. Petersburg as part of the centennial celebration of Major League Baseball in the city, image 2014. *Courtesy Michaels Family Collection.*

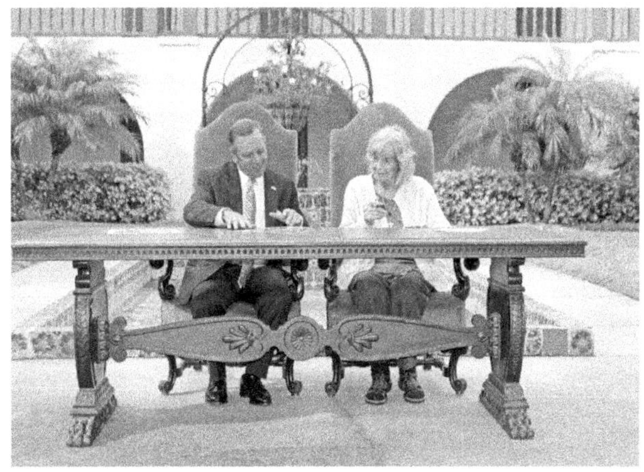

Julia Ruth Stevens and Stetson Law School dean Christopher M. Pietruszkiewicz during her 2014 visit to St. Petersburg. She is seated at the original table used by Babe Ruth and Jacob Ruppert at the Rolyat Hotel in St. Petersburg to sign Ruth's 1932 $75,000 contract with the Yankees, image 2014. *Courtesy Stetson Law School.*

> *I went back* [to the St. Pete Yacht Club] *in 1943 to be matron of honor for Pinky's wedding. That's the last time that I was in St. Pete. The only traveling that I do now is from here* [Henderson, Nevada] *back to Conway* [New Hampshire] *for the summer and the cooler weather, and I live here with my daughter-in-law and my son. They say,* "Mi casa, su casa."

Julia has spent summers in Conway since 1940.

Julia Ruth Stevens returned to St. Petersburg after seventy-one years in 2014 for the 100th Anniversary of Major League Spring Training. She threw the first pitch in the opening game of International Spring Training between Team Canada and the Baltimore Orioles, the Babe's first team. She was honored by a salute at Al Lang Stadium by representatives of the many charities Babe Ruth had supported when he spring trained in St. Pete, and she visited many of her Daddy's favorite places, including the Flori-de-Leon apartments, Huggins-Stengel Field at Crescent Lake, the Jungle Hotel (now Admiral Farragut Academy) and Stetson Law School, formerly the Rolyat Hotel. She stayed at the Renaissance Vinoy Hotel, another place her Daddy knew well.

Sources: George Beim with Julia Ruth Stevens, *Babe Ruth: A Daughter's Portrait* (1998); Julia Ruth Stevens and Bill Gilbert, *Babe Ruth: Remembering the Bambino in Stories, Photos and Memorabilia* (2008); and communications with Julia Ruth Stevens, Tom Stevens and Tim Reid.

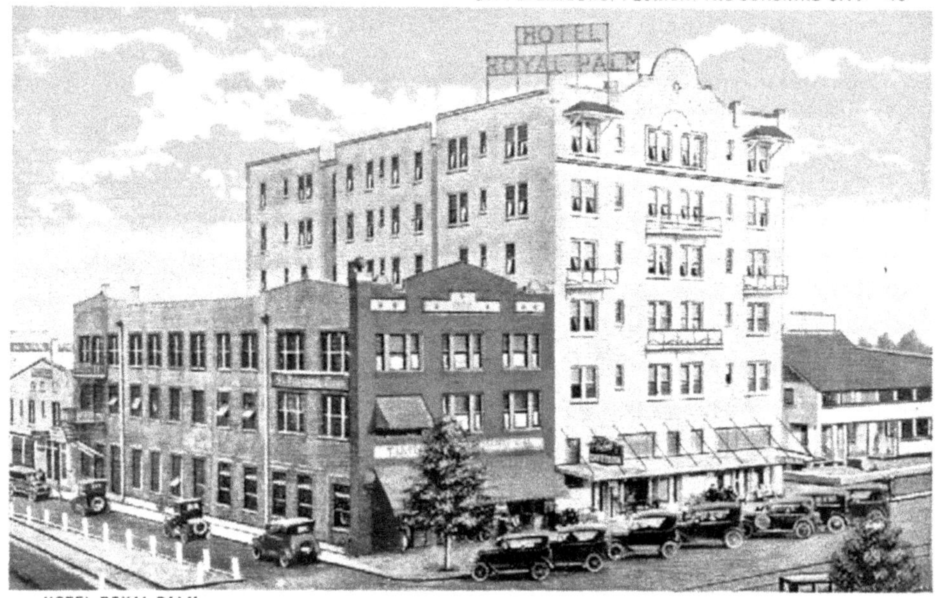

Al Capone was rumored to have stayed at the Royal Palm Hotel. Note that the hotel is adjacent to the St. Petersburg Times Building at the corner of 5th Street and 1st Avenue South (same location today). If he stayed at the Royal Palm, the paper reported nothing about it at the time, image circa 1930. *Courtesy Michaels Family Collection.*

Chapter 8

Al Capone in St. Petersburg

Much has been written about Al Capone, the notorious Chicago gangster. But Capone's association with St. Petersburg is truly part of our city's hidden history.

"Al Capone Pays Visit to the City" reads the caption on the front page of the *St. Petersburg Times* on February 10, 1931. The article reported:

> *Al "Scarface" Capone, reputed king of Chicago's gangland, paid a visit to Pinellas county Monday, spending a few hours in St. Petersburg and later motoring to Tarpon Springs, where he spent considerable time looking over the sponge industry. Capone, with a party of five, including one woman, was seen here by several persons. Later in the afternoon a large crowd gathered at the Sponge Exchange in Tarpon Springs to see the famous baronial head of the beer racket. Capone's business on Florida's west coast could not be ascertained, but there was plenty of speculation.*
>
> *...Some said he came to visit his old but retired henchman, John Torrio, who long ago settled down to a quiet life after a reputed "break" with "scarface." "There's nothing to that," a man at Torrio's home in a fashionable section here said Monday night. "Those two haven't seen each other for four years. Besides, John's in New York."*
>
> *...Capone was in St. Petersburg several years ago, stopping at a downtown hotel under the name of Al Brown, a moniker he discarded when he began his spectacular rise from a body guard for the late "Big Jim" Collissimio* [sic] *to his present position. Later he went to Miami, where he*

bought the big house on Palm island. Last year he was harassed by police and arrested time and time again. The governor issued an order forbidding him to enter the state, but this was staved off by a federal injunction. Capone and his party are making their trip over the state by motor.

Al Capone could well qualify as the most notorious gangster in American history. Starting out in Brooklyn as a youth in a local gang, he graduated to providing "muscle" in a protection racket operated by the Italian Five Points gang led by Paul Kelly and Johnny Torrio. Torrio had recruited Capone into the gang and publicly referred to him as his "nephew" although they were not related. Because of his smarts, Capone was promoted to bartender and bouncer in one of the gang's establishments. It was during this time that he was knifed in the face for insulting the sister of a patron, receiving his nickname, "Scarface." (Much later, he apologized to the knifer for insulting his sister and even hired him as an occasional bodyguard.) Subsequently, he became involved in a fight with a rival gang and may have fled to Chicago to avoid retaliation. Accounts of the exact circumstances of his relocation to Chicago differ, but Johnny Torrio himself had previously relocated to Chicago to join the gang of "Big Jim" Colosimo. Capone soon became a trusted lieutenant of Torrio and was a behind-the-scenes party to Torrio's subsequent murder of Big Jim. In January 1925, Torrio himself was the subject of a murder attempt by a rival gang. He received gunshot wounds to the arm, jaw, neck, chest and stomach and still managed to survive. Thereafter, he was known as "The Immune." It was then that he announced his retirement and turned his gang enterprises over to his second in command, Al Capone. But he continued to receive a cut of gang profits, perhaps as much as 25 percent, for ten years. He also was to be available for "consultations."

According to a 1925 *Chicago Daily Tribune* article, Torrio visited St. Pete in late 1924. Records verify that Torrio and his wife, Anna, traveled between Havana and Key West in December 1924. They made the same trip in November 1925 with Al Capone and his wife, Mary, also known as Mae. Capone's biographer, Robert Schoenberg, stated that after Torrio's retirement, he and his wife went to Italy for two years. Assuming he stayed in Italy the whole time would have him returning to the United States in about 1928. However, there are travel documents for John Torrio and his wife, Anna, giving St. Petersburg as their home address for the years 1926, 1927 and 1928. The documents were for travel between Hawaii and the West Coast. In May 1929, he was involved in organizing a loose cartel of Northeast bootleggers to prevent further turf wars. This evolved into what

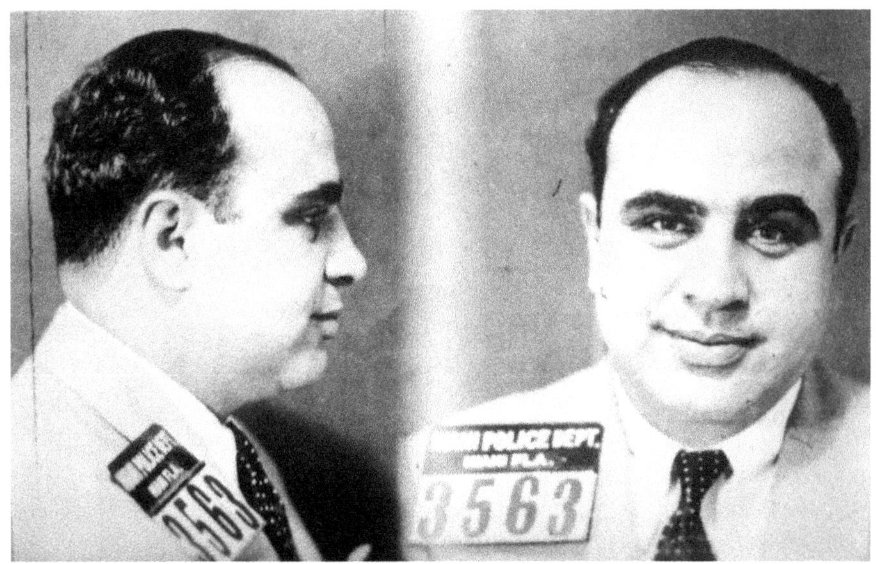

Mug shot of Al Capone taken in Miami, Florida. *Miami Police Department.*

became known as the National Crime Syndicate. Chicago newspaperman Fred Pasley stated that while Capone was in prison on a weapons possession charge in 1929, Torrio was based in Brooklyn but commuted twice a month to Chicago, likely assisting with running the Chicago operations in Capone's absence. Otherwise Torrio spent considerable time in real estate investments. Beginning in 1939, he served two years in prison for income tax evasion.

Torrio is identified as living in various St. Petersburg locations. These include 2300 Lakeview Avenue South (now 22nd Avenue South), possibly the 1600 block of Lakeview Avenue South, the 100 block of 14th Avenue Northeast, possibly another location in the Old Northeast neighborhood and Pass-a-Grille. Ship manifest documents for the Torrios give a 2300 Lakeview Avenue South address. City directories for 1925–28 list George R. Jacobs, or his mother, Belle, living at this address. George Jacobs was Anna Torrio's brother, and Belle Jacobs was her mother. In 1931, Anna's mother is listed as living at 14th Avenue Northeast. George Jacobs was a known Torrio associate.

There is an amusing story of Torrio on one occasion protecting a neighbor's pecan orchard from a poacher with a pruning axe near his residence on Lakeview Avenue. Torrio also sold (some accounts say "donated") property with a grove and large home known as the Green Cabin at 2350 Lakeview in 1927 to the American Legion for use as the original American Legion Hospital for Crippled Children, forerunner of today's All Children's Hospital. Today, the site of the American Legion Hospital and Torrio's 2300 Lakeview residence are the location of Sanderlin Middle School.

As Capone excelled in bootlegging, racketeering, vice, gambling and other organized crime, he made enemies. This resulted in much inter-gang carnage throughout the city of Chicago. Ultimately, Chicago mayor Bill Thompson, who was running for president at the time, ordered Capone out of the city. This was despite the fact that Thompson himself was on the take from Capone. It was at this moment that Capone made the only quote found mentioning St. Petersburg (December 5, 1927). "I'm leaving for St. Petersburg tomorrow," he said, further explaining that he had some property there he wanted to sell. As it turned out, the reference to St. Pete was a ruse, and instead he went to Tijuana, Mexico, and then Los Angeles, where he was again asked to leave town. But his reference to St. Petersburg is telling—a strange place to mention unless he had some connection to it.

Florida's governor also added his voice to the chorus declaring Capone unwelcome. *Chicago Tribune* newspaperman Fred Pasley, in his 1930 biography of Capone, stated that Capone did, in fact, go to St. Petersburg in early 1928 after his sojourn out west. Pasley wrote, "The police met him at the [train] station and trailed him so assiduously that he stayed only overnight." No local documentation of this has been found. Also, Capone was a fan of Babe Ruth, and some theorize that Capone came to St. Pete to see the Babe play in spring training games. But no documentation of this has been found either. Capone's wife stated in a 1941 deposition that Capone was in St. Pete for a "short visit…fourteen or fifteen years ago [1926 or '27]." After his possible brief stop in St. Petersburg, Capone went to Miami, and in March, he bought a fourteen-room estate on Palm Island. He called Florida "the garden of America, the sunny Italy of the new world, where life is good and abundant, where happiness is to be had even by the poorest."

February 14, 1929, was the date of the infamous Saint Valentine's Day Massacre. This involved the brutal execution of seven members of a rival Chicago gang. Capone is widely assumed to have been responsible for ordering the killings, although he personally had an alibi. He was in Miami meeting with an assistant district attorney from New York minutes after the slaughter occurred. The massacre attracted worldwide attention and further motivated public officials and law enforcement to bring Capone to justice.

In May 1929, Capone was convicted of possession of a weapon in Philadelphia and was sentenced to a year in prison, most of which he spent

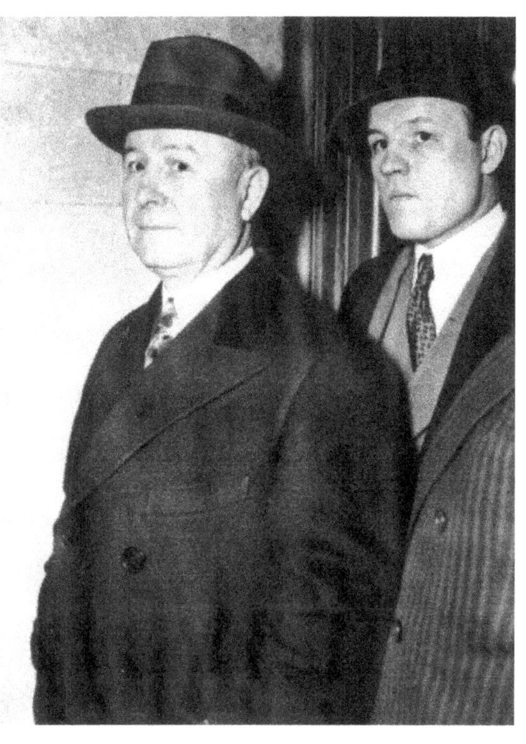

Mobster Johnny Torrio (left), together with Al Capone and other mobsters, invested extensively in St. Petersburg real estate.

at Eastern Penitentiary in Philadelphia. There Capone was allowed to furnish his cell, hire fellow prisoners as servants and receive many visitors and mail. The junk mail was thoughtfully discarded for Capone by the warden. He was released in March 1930, whereupon authorities in Chicago once more warned that he was unwelcome and that he would be arrested on sight if he entered the city. Florida's new governor, Doyle E. Carlton, followed suit. He sent an identical telegram to the sheriffs of all sixty-seven Florida counties: "It Is Reported that Al Capone Is on His Way to Florida. Arrest if He Comes Your Way and Escort to State Border with Instructions Not to Return. If You Need Additional Assistance Call Me." As if to help with Capone's public identification, *Time* magazine ran his photo on its cover for the March 24, 1930 edition.

Capone at some point attracted the active attention of President Hoover. Hoover repeatedly raised the issue of Capone's prosecution with his closest advisors after becoming president. Ultimately, the only charge the feds could get to stick against Capone was nonpayment of income tax, and even that was minimal. The indictment identified a little over $1 million in income between the years 1924 and 1929, for which $215,080 in taxes were owed. There is speculation that Johnny Torrio may have advised Capone to take the rap to get it over with, not expecting the long prison sentence he would receive. In May 1932, Capone was sent to the Atlanta Federal Prison. Having wised up to Capone and other criminals' ability to manipulate the prison system, in 1934 the government converted Alcatraz from a military to a federal maximum-security prison for the most dangerous criminals, including those with the resources to corrupt prison officials. Capone was among the first to be transferred there. Contrary to the experience a few years earlier in Philadelphia, Alcatraz was as grim as it got. There he occupied a nine- by five-foot cell. Personal furnishing was not permitted. Mail was heavily censored, and newspapers not allowed. Visitation was restricted to twice-a-month family visits. Use of personal funds to purchase anything was forbidden. He was paroled in 1939 and soon returned to his home in Palm Island, where he died of cardiac arrest in 1947, after a history of neurosyphilis that began to appear while he was in Alcatraz.

A 1961 *Times* editorial entitled "EVERYBODY'S TARGET: AL CAPONE" stated: "St. Petersburg and Pinellas County have been fortunate over their lifetime because our citizens have elected sheriffs and appointed police chiefs who have seen to it that racketeers moved on and never got a start here. That's the way the citizens wanted it when Pinellas broke away from Hillsborough 50 years ago and that's the way they want it today. In their heyday Al Capone, Johnny Torrio and other gangsters came to St. Petersburg, but their welcome was so cold and their stay so brief that the incident is hardly a footnote to history." Capone's visits to St. Pete may have been brief, but that was certainly not the case for Torrio, who wintered in the city for several years, starting perhaps as early as 1924 and certainly after 1925.

While Torrio enjoyed wintering in St. Pete's sunshine, that was not his only activity here. In addition to visiting his wife's brother and mother, he actively engaged in real estate speculation. This included a thirty-acre tract of land south of Lakeview Avenue (now 22nd Avenue and in the vicinity of the Twin Brooks Golf Course); North Disston Boulevard (now 49th Street); Lido Beach, Sarasota; various properties along Central Avenue; 4th Street North in the vicinity of 7th Avenue; and property in Pass-a-Grille. The Pass-a-Grille property was sold in 1945 to Sheriff Hugh Culbreath of Hillsborough County and became the subject of an inquiry by the Kefauver Senate Crime Committee in 1950. Interestingly, a descendant of the founder of Rhodes Funeral Home on 4th Street North reported his father buying the property from Al Capone's son-in-law in 1925. Capone did not have a son-in-law then, but possibly the property was purchased from Torrio or one of his associates.

To what extent Capone had an interest in some of these properties is harder to document. The Ken Burns and Lynn Novick documentary *Prohibition* stated that Capone did not link his name to real estate, and documentation of Capone's St. Petersburg real estate investments from original records has not been established. County officials state that tax records do not go back that far. But Capone's name was reported in newspaper accounts to be on the tax records for the Twin Brooks and Disston parcels. A December 18, 1965 *Independent* article reported that Capone operated under the auspices of the Manro Corporation, which was jointly owned by Torrio, Capone, Jake ("Jack") Guzik and Jack Vanella. A 1957 *St. Petersburg Times* article stated that tax records showed Capone owned eighteen acres south of Lakewood Avenue. Jack Guzik owned additional property nearby. Guzik was Torrio's accountant when he was active in Chicago and later continued on as a financial advisor to Capone. Jack Vanella was identified in the press as a representative of Capone. Other press accounts refer to a Robert Vanella. Robert "Roxie" Vanella was a criminal associate of Torrio. Capone also reportedly owned property with Torrio on Central Avenue. A 1926 Shore Acres home has been rumored to have been built by Capone, possibly for his mother. But no evidence of this has been found. His mother lived in Chicago, occasionally visiting Capone's Miami Beach home. In 1936, Capone paid $51,489 to clear U.S. liens against his Florida property, including that in St. Petersburg. A 1931 *Independent* article reflected, "In the time he was living here Torrio has been very little in evidence and only a few people ever saw him to know him [*sic*] though it was generally known that he was living here. Torrio's name has never been connected here with anything other than legitimate business transactions." Also, the *Tampa Tribune* noted that "his chief recreation seemed to be feeding pigeons in Williams Park and tossing small coins to children."

Gangsters have been reported as guests at various St. Petersburg–area hotels. A 1992 *Times* article leads off, "AL CAPONE BATHED HERE!" The article quotes *Times* writer Dick Bothwell as saying that the Royal Palm Hotel was a stopping place for Capone and some of his "cohorts" in 1926. The hotel once stood at 112 5th Street South. It was demolished in about 1967 to make way for the expansion of the Times Building. Direct documentation of Bothwell's alleged statement has not been found. However, a 1974 *Times* article referred to the Royal Palm story as a "rumor" and added that Capone supposedly stayed at the hotel for two days and registered as "A. Brown," an alias he frequently used. Perhaps the basis for Bothwell's possible assertion was the 1931 *Times* article quoted earlier. Sometimes rumors have a kernel of truth. It may be that the date 1926 was an error but that other elements of the story were correct. A better alternative date might be 1928, the date mentioned by Pasley for a brief visit after Capone's first eviction from Chicago.

A popular St. Pete ghost story book claims that Capone, his family and "henchmen" stayed at the Sunset Hotel at the west end of Central Avenue near Boca Ciega Bay. It's possible that Capone or his associates may have stayed there, although adding his family is a stretch. The Sunset Hotel would have been convenient to the famous Gang Plank Night Club and other sources of liquor and vice in the area. But no documentation of a Capone association has been found.

At one time the Don CeSar Hotel claimed on its website that Al Capone stayed there, but that has been removed. However, Jean Renwick Ott, an assistant to the Don's developer, Thomas J. Rowe, recalled in a 1988 interview that when the hotel first opened in about 1928, she met "shady friends of gangster Al Capone, who also owned property in St. Petersburg Beach." As for the Vinoy Park Hotel (now the Renaissance Vinoy), the hotel's in-house historian stated that she had no knowledge of Capone ever staying there.

Historian Scott Taylor Hartzell wrote in a *Times* column that the Jungle Hotel, now Admiral Farragut Academy, entertained "henchmen for Al Capone." Walter P. Fuller built and owned the Jungle Country Club Hotel and nearby Gangplank Nightclub, conveniently located on Boca Ciega Bay, where it was easy to offload whiskey from bootleg boats. Fuller in later life freely admitted to being a bootlegger. "I, a nondrinker at the advent of Prohibition [1920] became a lawbreaker, a habitual evader of authority and a steady customer of alcoholic beverages," he stated in 1970. "The first bootlegger I ever saw was me. In such an atmosphere, even the most righteous lacked the courage to speak out, and law enforcers became a lonely and ostracized group." Fuller was not only a leading St. Petersburg developer, but he also later went on to become an able state legislator and writer of a city history. Fuller opened the Jungle Hotel in February 1926. He noted that some of Chicago's criminal element visited the hotel, including Johnny Torrio. "They were the most genteel, the best mannered guests."

A September 28, 1974 unattributed *Times* article in the "Scene Action" column stated that Torrio came to St. Petersburg in 1925 as Capone's "front man." It then went on to say that "[a]lthough the Torrios lived here for a year or so, we find no record of home ownership. The whole Capone crew stayed at the late Walter Fuller's hotel [in 1926?]...during an abortive attempt to operate a gambling ship just beyond the three-mile limit." The article further quoted Fuller as saying that after Capone was arrested in 1926, Torrio left immediately and never returned. What arrest is being referred to is unknown. Additionally, it was reported that Capone was a party to several real estate investments and that Fuller was convinced Capone never visited

St. Pete personally. In 1967, Fuller wrote a letter that stated, "Absolutely, positively, unequivocally and beyond a peradventure of doubt for sure, Al Capone was never in St. Petersburg." Apparently, Fuller did not see the front-page story in the *Times* about Capone's "few hours" spent in St. Pete in 1931 or did not think that counted.

During Capone's February 1931 visit to the area, the *Times* also reported that Capone and his associates visited the Clearwater Court House, where an associate discussed St. Petersburg's Club Madrid, recently raided by police. Capone did not engage in the conversation but waited in his car. Club Madrid was located near the Jungle Prado Night Club, also operated by Walter Fuller.

So was Al Capone really in St. Petersburg, and if so, what was he doing here? Based on the 1931 *Times* article, we know that Capone spent at least a few hours in St. Petersburg before proceeding to Tarpon Springs on February 9, 1931. A local Tarpon Springs paper also covered the 1931 visit. That paper asserted that Capone spent "several days" in St. Petersburg. Additionally, it appears that Capone paid at least one visit to St. Pete sometime between 1926 and 1928. Only Chicago journalist and biographer Fred Pasley reported a definite year: 1928. But Pasley's biography of Capone has its problems. No local confirmation has been found that Capone was met at the train station upon his arrival in St. Pete by police who "trailed him assiduously," as Pasley asserted. Surely Capone's arrival would have been a newsworthy event. With his extensive facial scars, he would have been hard not to notice. Pasley's narrative needs to be read with skepticism. It's possible that he received information directly from Capone that was spun to protect Capone's (and Torrio's) interests. In this regard, Pasley made no mention of Torrio's frequent presence in St. Petersburg. Perhaps Capone was in St. Pete in 1928 but was not greeted by police. And perhaps he spent two nights at the Royal Palm Hotel, as referenced in the 1931 *Times* article and later allegedly reported by *Times* columnist Dick Bothwell, rather than one night, as stated by Pasley.

And the purpose of Capone's possible 1928 trip? The most compelling theory would be to consult with his mentor and silent partner Johnny Torrio. Unfortunately, we have no confirmation of whether Torrio was in the city at that particular time, although we know he was a visitor or part-time resident from the mid-1920s into the 1930s. At the time of the possible 1928 visit, Capone had not quite yet bought his home in Palm Island at Miami Beach and had not yet reached the peak of his notoriety.

Capone's grandniece Deirdre Marie Capone reported that after Capone purchased his home at Palm Island in 1928, he would on occasion drive from Chicago to Miami via Route 41, which would have taken him through the Tampa Bay area. Rather than meetings in St. Petersburg, a safer option would have been for Torrio to go to Capone for consultations or just a friendly visit in Tampa, Miami (or elsewhere). Miami was very friendly to Capone, and meeting there would have less chance of jeopardizing Torrio's low profile in St. Petersburg. Of course, it's possible that Capone was in St. Pete on other occasions as yet lost to history.

Finally, there is the matter of Torrio's and Capone's extensive real estate investments in St. Petersburg and other nearby areas. Given Torrio's semi-retirement, jumping into the 1920s St. Pete land boom, or even after the boom ended in 1927, makes some sense as a financial investment. Capone's investing is harder to fathom. Did he really need the money? Perhaps he was doing it as a favor to his mentor. Were these investments an early form of money laundering? Perhaps the real estate investments were simply a part of a larger effort to diversify from his illicit liquor operations. Perhaps another purpose of the investments was to secure St. Petersburg as a safe haven for Torrio. As the 1931 *Independent* article noted, few people knew that Torrio had made St. Petersburg his seasonal home. Did his extensive financial investments in the community somehow help avoid closer local scrutiny? And how significant were these investments in fueling the local land boom or softening the impact of the subsequent depression?

Much has been written about the 1920s St. Petersburg boom era. It was a period of astronomical building growth; get-rich-quick real estate dealing; glorious new hotels such as the Soreno, Vinoy, Don CeSar, Rolyat and the Jungle; the five-mile Gandy Bridge connecting to Tampa and the Bee Line Ferry connecting to the South; rampant tourism; minimal enforcement of Prohibition; and just plain zaniness. Celebrities came to the city both to perform and to vacation: novelist F. Scott Fitzgerald; criminal defense attorney Clarence Darrow; bandleader John Philip Sousa; golf champions Walter Hagen and Gene Sarazen; baseball icons Babe Ruth, Lou Gehrig and Tony Lazzeri; and entertainers Harry James, Rudy Valee, Will Rogers and Sophie Tucker, to name a few. Historian Raymond Arsenault wrote that during the 1920s, "the city flirted with decadence" and that there was "a new looseness in social mores." Maybe the city did more than flirt, as it also attracted celebrities of a different ilk, such as Johnny Torrio and Al Capone.

Mobsters usually do not disclose their operations, and what they do disclose is often disinformation. No doubt the full story of Torrio's presence and Capone's influence in St. Petersburg remains to be discovered.

Sources: Raymond Arsenault, *St. Petersburg and the Florida Dream: 1888–1950* (1988/1996); Prudy Taylor Board, *The Renaissance Vinoy: St. Petersburg's Crown Jewel* (1999); Stephen C. Bousquet, "The Gangster in Our Midst: Al Capone in South Florida, 1930–1947," *Florida Historical Quarterly* 76, no. 3 (Winter, 1998): 297–308; Deirdre Marie Capone, *Uncle Al Capone: The Untold Story from Inside His Family* (2012); *Chicago Daily Tribune*, January 25, 1925; *Clearwater Sun*, February 10, 1931; Kim Cool, *Ghost Stories of Clearwater and St. Petersburg* (2004); Scott Deitche, "Al Capone in St. Petersburg," *Informer* (October 2012): 4–10; *Evening Independent*, various dates but especially March 15, 1978; Scott Taylor Hartzell, *Remembering St. Petersburg* (2006), vol. 2; Scott Taylor Hartzell, *St. Petersburg: An Oral History* (2002); Sally J. Ling, *Al Capone's Miami: Paradise or Purgatory* (2015); Gary R. Mormino, "Tampa at Mid Century: 1950," *Sunland Tribune* (journal of the Tampa Historical Society) 26 (2000): 65–81; Fred D. Pasley, *Al Capone: The Biography of a Self-Made Man* (1930); *St. Petersburg Times*, various dates but especially February 10, 1931, February 13, 1931, January 13, 1939, February 13, 1961, September 28, 1974, January 17, 1988, March 23, 1992, November 19, 1994, December 12, 2009; Robert J. Schoenberg, *Mr. Capone* (1992); June Hurley Young, *The Don Ce-Sar Story* (Partnership Press, n.d.); *Tarpon Springs Leader*, February 10, 1931; and communications with Deirdre Marie Capone, Scott Deitche, Elaine Normile, Kimberly Hinder and Gary Mormino.

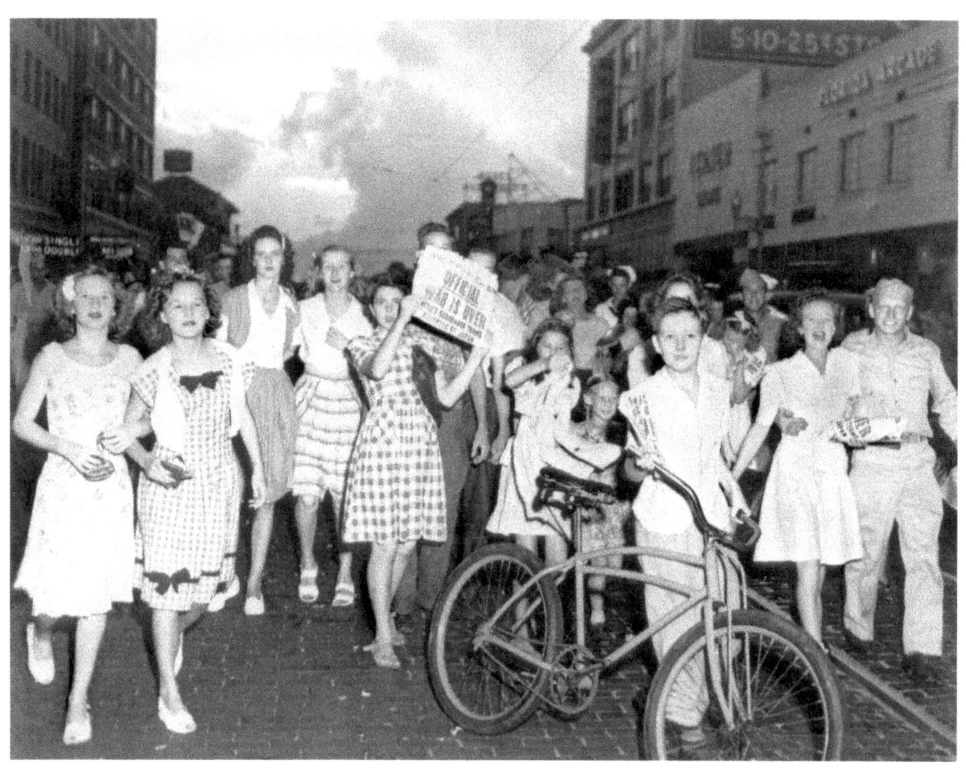

V-J Day (Victory Over Japan) celebration on Central Avenue, August 14, 1945. *Courtesy St. Petersburg Museum of History.*

Chapter 9

St. Petersburg Conquers World War II

As in the rest of the country, World War II was a painful and difficult time for St. Petersburg and its people. More than 8,000 local residents served in the armed services during the war, including nearly two thousand African Americans. Many of those going into the armed services made the ultimate sacrifice. Others were maimed and wounded. Additionally, another 3,700 union mechanics left St. Petersburg to work in war plants.

Food and goods of all types were rationed. Only five gallons of gas were allowed per week, and maximum speed was limited to thirty-five miles per hour. A rigid blackout was enforced. The city joined the rest of the country in declaring "Meatless Tuesdays." Civilians positioned on the roof of the Vinoy Park Hotel served as enemy plane spotters. The "Bomb-a-Dears" were formed by young ladies from local high schools and the Junior College to entertain the troops.

Replacing a Tourist Economy

St. Petersburg was particularly challenged as a city because it was primarily a tourist economy, and with the coming of the war, that economy collapsed. Within a few months after Pearl Harbor, the city's hotels and boardinghouses were nearly empty. As historian Raymond Arsenault noted, "Few cities felt the winds of war as early as St. Petersburg, and even fewer underwent such a thoroughgoing militarization."

Local leaders anticipated the coming of the war, and this caused them to pause and take stock. What could be done with St. Petersburg's many tourist hotels and the infrastructure supporting them? Then someone had an idea. Why not present St. Petersburg with its vast network of hotels, cafeterias, recreational facilities and other amenities as a training site for the expansion of our armed services? An aggressive campaign led by the chamber of commerce, city officials and Congressman J. Harden Peterson convinced Washington to act.

Army Air Corps Leads the Way

The War Department selected St. Petersburg as a major technical services training center for the U.S. Army Air Corps. Using the Vinoy Park Hotel as its headquarters, the U.S. Air Corps leased every major hotel in the city, except the Suwannee. The Suwannee was kept for what little business trade remained. Dozens of smaller hotels were also leased.

But even this was not enough to house the influx of troops. Many were forced to pitch their tents on hotel grounds or in city parks. At the height of the influx in late 1942, about 10,000 soldiers were camped at the Piper-Fuller airport next to the Jungle Country Club golf course (parts of the area we now know as Azalea and Tyrone). By the time the army air corps training center was discontinued in July 1943, approximately 120,000 trainees and instructors had seen St. Petersburg.

In addition to the army air corps, there was the Coast Guard and the United States Maritime Service. Responsibility for training merchant seamen was transferred from the Coast Guard to the Maritime Service in the summer of 1942. The number of seamen trainees also ballooned, and the base at Bayboro Harbor was expanded. The Maritime Service eventually leased four of the downtown hotels previously used by the air corps. By war's end, more than twenty-five thousand merchant seamen had been trained.

Other military organizations to locate in the area included a navy anti-submarine base at Bayboro, a coastal artillery battery at Pass-a-Grille on the barrier islands and a convalescent hospital at the Don CeSar Hotel—where Cary Grant once entertained and baseball star Joe DiMaggio was stationed. A small air corps training facility was located at Albert Whitted Airport, and there was a larger center at the Pinellas Army Air Base, site of present-day St. Petersburg–Clearwater Airport. Mullet Key (Fort De Soto) was used as a bombing practice site, leaving several unexploded bombs to be discovered as late at 1988.

Hotels at Pass-a-Grille were insufficient for the coastal artillery battery, so a number of homes were occupied there as well. St. Petersburg Beach historian

Frank Hurley noted that the GIs swarmed over the beaches on their time off. "Beach bars never had it so good. Even today, barkeeps who went through it get misty-eyed when they remember those clanging cash registers." In addition to soldiers actually based in St. Petersburg, thousands of other soldiers on pass from Tampa and Hillsborough County visited St. Petersburg and its beaches.

Beach areas were particularly fearful of German submarines off the coast. Cars had to be parked at least one block back from the beach, facing away from the Gulf so as to avoid shining headlights toward the water. All house windows facing the Gulf had to be shielded so no light would show. Local resident Betsy Pheil related how her family was under suspicion during the war because of their German name. This was despite the fact that her grandfather Abe Pheil was an early St. Petersburg mayor. Betsy's father, Harvey ("Hops") Pheil, owned beachfront property. On one occasion when he wiped the perspiration off his forehead with a white handkerchief while at his beach place, neighbors called the police because they thought he was signaling to a German submarine.

The presence of the troops also attracted a large number of military wives to the area. Many left after their husbands were shipped out, but others stayed behind to wait out the war in tropical St. Petersburg. All of this created a shortage of local housing. While the 1940 census showed a population of 60,000 in St. Petersburg, the wartime population probably swelled to in excess of 100,000.

NANCY OSMON HAAK

Many local residents who experienced the war years in St. Petersburg still reside here. Nancy Osmon Haak is a lifelong resident of St. Petersburg. Her parents were Orin and Edna Osmon. They came to St. Petersburg from southern Illinois in 1924. At that time, it took ten days to make the trip. Orin was a painter who, at one time, worked on the decorative beams at Bay Pines Veterans Hospital. Edna was the manager of the famous Solarium on the Pier for thirty-four years. The Solarium was known at the time as the world's best-equipped open-air sun bathing facility. Nudity was permitted for medicinal purposes.

Even though Nancy was only seven years old at the time, she distinctly remembered Pearl Harbor. She was playing in front of her house with two other little girls. When she returned to her front porch, her dad was there. He had apparently heard about the bombing of Pearl Harbor on the radio and told her that he and her brother "would have to fight a war." The next day, her dad went down to the draft board with his friends. To his consternation, he was rejected for service but immediately became an air raid warden.

Everyone was encouraged to take a Red Cross first aide course, and all of us children were asked to collect tin cans, scrap, and grease…Many houses had a flag with a little star, which meant someone at that house was in the service. Everyone was excited to receive a letter from a family member in the service but upset when key parts of the letter had been cut out by the censors. There were pup tents pitched at the Rolyat Hotel, and the soldiers would march down 5th Avenue and Park Street. Others would march near the Vinoy. Spa Beach near the Pier would be packed with soldiers sunbathing and swimming. People were discouraged from going to the beaches at Pass-a-Grille and St. Petersburg Beach. For one thing, the trolley did not go that far, and gas was in short supply to drive. My mother worked at the Solarium. She brought many young soldiers home to share Sunday dinner.

VE Day [Victory in Europe] *was exciting. We lived at 17th Street and 3rd Avenue North at the time. We knew the end of the war was coming, but no plans were made for a celebration. Everyone went downtown to Central Avenue. There was bumper-to-bumper traffic with horns tooting. It had been a long time since there were so many cars on the street, and it was strange to see. My mother and father had been given twenty-five silver dollars for their anniversary. Now that the war was over, they took them out*

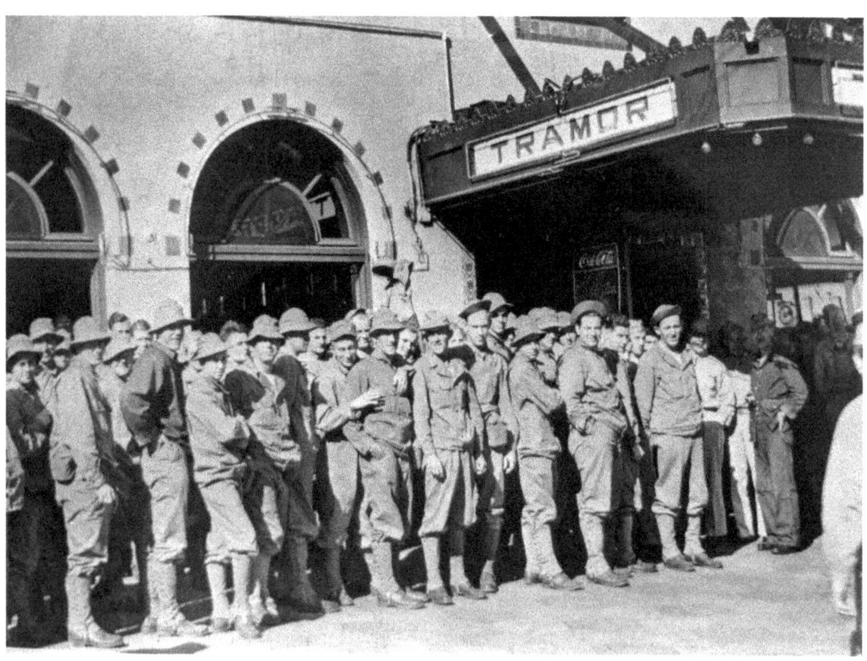

During World War II, St. Petersburg became a vast training facility for the military. Hotels were used for barracks, and cafeterias became mess halls. Here troops line up outside the Tramor Cafeteria for supper, image 1943. *Courtesy St. Petersburg Museum of History.*

of the safety deposit box where they had been saving them. My mother used them to buy a mix-master, and my father used them to buy some new tires.

TURNING POINT

World War II was an obvious turning point for St. Petersburg. The experience of war leaves an impact both at the front and at home. But there were special impacts on St. Petersburg. Prior to the war, the city's population had begun to age. As of 1940, much of the city's youthful image from the Roaring Twenties had diminished. With the coming of the military, youth were back at center stage. The traditional social roles of women began to change as they, along with teens and retirees, picked up the jobs previously done by young men. For the first time, the city hired women to run the buses and trolleys, and some women were even hired as laborers by the railroad. Racism was also tempered somewhat because the country was fighting a foe that took racism to its ultimate conclusion. The American government's anti-Nazi information programs helped to discredit extreme racism. Economically, the city and nearby areas did very well. Even the Vinoy Park Hotel was able to pay off its mortgage with the money generated from its lease with the War Department.

Because of the war, thousands of veterans saw St. Petersburg who otherwise would not have, and most liked what they saw. After the war, thousands returned to the city, some as tourists but many to stay and make the city their home. This mass in-migration of veterans and their families sparked a major postwar building boom. Of equal significance, earlier booms had been driven by investment in empty lots. This boom was driven by actual housing needs. By 1950, the city's population had increased from sixty thousand people in 1940 to nearly ninety-seven thousand.

As Arsenault stated, "World War II proved to be a major watershed in the city's history. Many people had the profound sense that nearly everything was different after the war, and they were right. In countless ways the war accelerated technological and social change, propelling the city and the nation into a new age."

Sources: Raymond Arsenault, *St. Petersburg and the Florida Dream: 1888–1950* (1988/1996); Rick Baker, *Mangroves to Major League* (2000); Prudy Taylor Board, *The Renaissance Vinoy: St. Petersburg's Crown Jewel* (1999); Walter P. Fuller, *St. Petersburg and Its People* (1972); Frank T. Hurley Jr., *Surf, Sand, & Post Card Sunsets: A History of Pass-a-Grille and the Gulf Beaches* (1977/1989); Karl H. Grismer, *The Story of St. Petersburg* (1948); and interviews with Nancy Osmon Haak and Betsy Pheil.

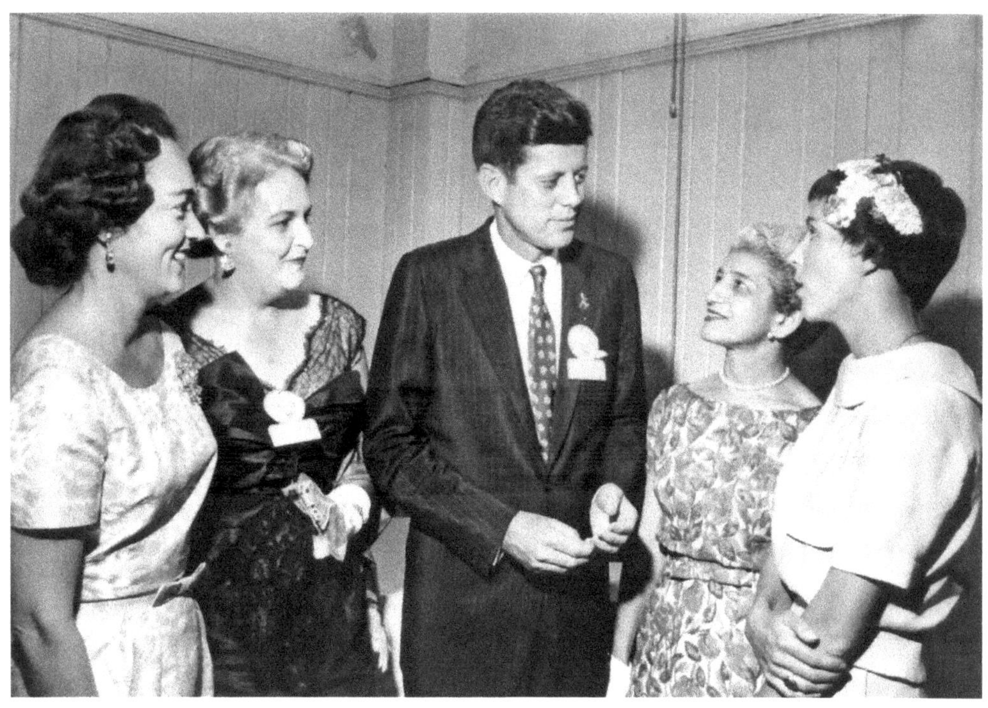

John F. Kennedy campaigning at the Historic Detroit Hotel, image 1959. *Courtesy St. Petersburg Museum of History.*

Chapter 10

Election Times

1952–1984

The 1952 elections were a landslide for Eisenhower. Nationally, he won with 55 percent of the popular vote and took thirty-nine of the forty-eight states, including Florida. General Dwight David Eisenhower was a war hero—Supreme Allied Commander in Europe during World War II. His opponent was Adlai Stevenson, governor of Illinois. If 55 percent was a landslide nationally, the vote for Eisenhower in St. Petersburg was a raging flood. He received approximately 71 percent of the vote and carried all but seven of fifty-one precincts. The few precincts he did not carry were largely in the African American community. St. Petersburg returned to its Republican sympathies after the long dry spell of the Roosevelt years in 1948, when Dewey beat Truman in St. Pete, and the GOP local win in 1952 further confirmed this. Further, many servicemen who had trained in St. Petersburg during World War II returned to the city to live after the war. This no doubt helped further boost Eisenhower's vote. Herman Goldner, mayor of St. Petersburg from 1961 to 1967 and again from 1971 to 1973, served as West Coast chair of "Florida for Eisenhower." Half of the polling places in the city were at garages or filling stations such as Ted's Super Service Station on 1st Avenue North. Others were at fire stations, the Little Theater and the Masonic Home.

The Republicans also took most open offices in Pinellas County. Republican Congressional candidate and attorney William C. Cramer lost by a whisker to Dunedin businessman Courtney Campbell, after whom the Courtney Campbell Causeway between Tampa and Clearwater was named. Pinellas County experienced the third-highest county voter turnout in Florida, with 79 percent of those registered voting. This represented 64 percent of all persons over twenty-one years of age. By comparison, 74 percent of registered voters participated in the 2012 election.

Two days before the election, Tennessee senator Estes Kefauver arrived in St. Petersburg to stump for the Democrats. Kefauver himself was a candidate for the Democratic nomination but lost to Stevenson. In a rally at Williams Park, he praised General Eisenhower as an outstanding military man and then added, "I hope he will still be one after Nov. 4th." On election day, Eisenhower stated, "Win, lose, or draw, our job is America." The *St. Petersburg Times* endorsed the Democratic candidate but further stated, "Whomever [*sic*] is elected President today is going to need the united support of all people. Neither this nation nor the free world can afford the luxury of our remaining divided in the face of the threat of Communist imperialism." The paper went on to praise a local tradition that the *Times* and radio station WTSP had initiated, the "Winners-Losers Party." This was an actual party held after the election for winners and losers to come together, break the ice and move-on.

1956 ELECTION

The 1956 election again pitted Eisenhower against Stevenson, and Ike again won by a landslide. Nationally, he did even better than in 1952, capturing 57 percent of the popular vote and forty-one of the forty-eight states, again including Florida. Vice President Richard M. Nixon made a campaign stop at Al Lang Stadium in September. In St. Petersburg, Eisenhower slightly improved his margin, winning approximately 72 percent of the vote. This time he carried every precinct in the city. In 1952, the precinct located at Fire Station No. 3 at 5th Avenue and 27th Street South, for example, tilted for Stevenson. In 1956, it went for Eisenhower by 73 percent. The number of persons voting in 1956 increased by 31 percent over 1952, reflecting the city's growing population. The turnout was so massive that it overtaxed the voting machines in many precincts. Lines were long, and many voters gave up waiting. Some reported standing in line for more than two hours. While some people zipped through the machines in thirty to forty seconds, "others practically had to be drug out."

In an editorial after the election, the *Times* attributed the Republican Party's gains primarily to Eisenhower's personal popularity. "Republicans—

without Eisenhower—would not have made an impressive showing in the state. Their slogans and chanting went too far and led to blind straight voting." It bemoaned that in 1954 Republicans had cast "69,852 votes in Florida for a candidate for governor…who had been dead for several weeks, but whose name had not been scratched from the ballot." In Pinellas County, only three Democrats were elected in 1956: the sheriff, the superintendent of schools and the tax collector. Republican Congressional candidate William Cramer, who ran in 1952 and lost, unseated Courtney Campbell in 1954. He was the first Florida Republican elected to Congress since 1880. He again won in 1956, this time with the *Times*' endorsement. The paper again noted that the Democratic Party would do better when it "[does] not have to compete against the personal popularity of an Eisenhower," provided the Democrats had the "drive and sinew to build a loyal opposition."

One bright spot for the *Times* at the state level was the reelection of State Representative John B. Orr. Orr was from Dade County and a severe critic of the state legislature's efforts to circumvent the Supreme Court's 1954 *Brown v. Board of Education* decision declaring segregated schools illegal. Orr had declared on the floor of the House, "I believe segregation is morally wrong." He subsequently dealt with threats on his family and an unusually tough battle for reelection. The *Times* asserted its belief that "desegregation is inevitable" and applauded the many Floridians who supported Orr's stand. The director of the Florida Negro Voters League acknowledged a major shift by Florida African American voters to the Republican candidate in the 1956 election. The *Brown* decision, led by Eisenhower-appointed Supreme Court justice Earl Warren, was no doubt a major reason for this. There was also resentment regarding Democratic Mississippi senator James Eastland's outspoken opposition to the *Brown* decision. In 1957, Eisenhower further asserted his commitment to civil rights with the 1957 Civil Rights Act and by sending federal troops to support integration in Little Rock, Arkansas.

One curiosity during the campaign occurred in September. Dr. Paul F. Wallace, a St. Petersburg auto hobbyist, purchased the White House limousine that had been used by Franklyn Roosevelt, Harry Truman and Eisenhower. The limo was dubbed the "Queen Mary" and came with a gun cabinet for submachine guns. Dr. Wallace drove the limo from Washington to St. Pete.

1960 ELECTION

The Twenty-second Amendment to the U.S. Constitution, limiting presidential terms to no more than two, took effect in 1951. This prevented Eisenhower from running again. Given his heart attack in 1955 and general health, he probably would not have run again even if he could have. Vice President Richard M. Nixon of California stepped up to become the Republican candidate in 1960. His Democratic opponent was the junior senator from Massachusetts John F. Kennedy. In October, Nixon campaigned in St. Petersburg at Al Lang Field with a giant poster of Nixon shaking his finger at Soviet premier Nikita Khrushchev. He was received by local Republican VIPs at the Ponce de Leon Hotel and serenaded with "Dixie" by the Dixieland Yanks. On the same day Nixon spoke in St. Petersburg, his rival Kennedy appeared in Tampa. The *Times* marked the occasion with an extensive editorial extending a "warm welcome" to the two candidates. It stated that "it was here in Pinellas, and spreading out from here up and down the coast, that the two-party system had its real genesis in the South. Nor is this accidental, nor because of the pattern of immigration to this area. For two decades there has been a deliberate attempt—and this newspaper has been one of its prime movers—to develop a new political consciousness and maturity here." It noted that Pinellas County had become a "spring training ground" for aspirants to the presidency and that the Democratic primaries no longer determined election for local office. It said the effect of these changes "on Southern politics and government will be profound. In the long run it should mean better government at all levels. And at the national level it should mean a new respect and consideration for the South and its problems." Kennedy had campaigned in St. Petersburg in 1959.

Kennedy won the national election with 49.7 percent of the popular vote, edging out Nixon by two-tenths of 1 percent. However, he collected 58 percent of the electoral vote. Pinellas County and St. Petersburg continued in their Republican tradition. Nixon swept the county with 63 percent of the vote. Beginning with the 1960 election, voting data broken out for St. Petersburg cannot be found and would require a detailed precinct analysis to determine. The focus was on the county level of government. Since St. Petersburg was the largest city in Pinellas County by far, the vote at the county level is generally indicative of that in the city. A perusal of precinct data for St. Petersburg shows St. Petersburg following suit with the county. Kennedy carried only nine precincts, primarily in African American neighborhoods.

The *Times* again supported the Democratic candidate for president, but at the state and local level, it included a number of Republicans among its endorsements. The Republicans were elected at the local level, but none of the Democrats. Total votes cast in Pinellas hit a record 160,000, greatly exceeding the 1956 level of 102,000. Nixon also carried Florida by 52 percent, and the Republicans were competitive, although not victorious, at state level offices. It would be another six years before the first Republican governor since Reconstruction, Claude Kirk, would be elected. Republicans would not dominate the state House and Senate until the 1990s. The *Times* editorially summed up the election: "[T]he main theme at this time for the Democrats in Florida is that things will never again be the same politically, which is well and good, assuming of course, that there is both a realization and adjustment to it." It suggested that elections be staggered so that in years when a president is elected, "this major solemn decision can be made without the distractions of long listings of other candidates and propositions."

1964 ELECTION

Kennedy was assassinated shortly after a visit to Tampa in 1963, where among other things he led the celebration of the fiftieth anniversary of the world's first airline and its pilot, Tony Jannus. Vice President Lyndon Baines Johnson ("LBJ") then assumed the presidency. Johnson ran in his own right in 1964 against Senator Barry Goldwater of Arizona. Goldwater paid a visit to St. Petersburg on September 15, speaking to twelve thousand people at Al Lang Stadium. The following month saw LBJ's vice presidential candidate, Hubert Humphrey, speak at Williams Park. He was introduced by city mayor Herman Goldner, a Republican who supported Johnson.

In the 1964 election, voters had to pull sixty-two levers in the voting machine if they were to vote for every office and proposition. And they were allowed by law only five minutes to do it. Expecting long lines and waits, they were advised by the *Times* to "tuck a fried egg sandwich in your pocket upon leaving the house, or a jug of lemonade" and to have some interesting stories "other than politics" to tell fellow line standers.

Johnson prevailed at the national level with 61 percent of the popular vote—the highest ever attained. He carried Florida and all but six states. He also carried Pinellas County with 55 percent of the vote. This was the first time a Democratic presidential candidate had carried Pinellas since Franklin

Roosevelt in 1944. Exact figures are not available for St. Petersburg, but again the vote there generally followed the county. Johnson benefited from heavy votes in predominantly black voting precincts, no doubt influenced in part by his advocacy for and signing in July of the landmark Civil Rights Act outlawing major forms of segregation, including inequality in voter registration requirements and racial segregation in schools. His opponent, Goldwater, had voted against the act, saying he saw it as an intrusion of state's and personal rights.

The Democrats made significant gains in local offices, although Republican congressman Cramer was reelected by a sizable margin. Active Democrat and local historian Walter P. Fuller commented that the reason the Democrats in Pinellas and Florida did well "was because they finally had the guts to recognize the national ticket." This was a reference to Democrats holding back in 1960 because of Kennedy's Catholic religion. Fuller also noted that the Democrats had money and good candidates. On the other hand, he stated that the Republicans were divided locally and nationally. "They were in a state of turmoil. You don't win elections that way." Contrary to what the *Times* had editorialized just four years before, in 1964 it attributed the local Democratic victory to a slowdown in in-migration to the county. It stated that the great influx of new residents since World War II had been dominating local elections. These new residents, not knowing local candidates or problems, simply voted for candidates of the party with which they had previously been affiliated. "This had the double effect of putting in office some miserably weak candidates and discouraging good Democratic candidates from offering themselves."

Republican congressman Cramer also blamed the local Republican defeat on "straight Democratic voting in the Negro precincts" and Democrats having more money. One reason for the straight voting may have been Republican "Operation Eagle Eye." Under this program, the Republicans placed teams of poll-watchers in many precincts for the stated reason of preventing illegal voting. St. Petersburg African American attorney and chair of the Pinellas County Voter Education Committee James B. Sanderlin remarked that many blacks "got nervous from the hostility of some of the challenges and forgot the Republicans they wanted to vote for....I think that in the voters' minds the Republicans became the hostile enemy—someone trying to deprive them of their vote. I attribute that to the lack of ticket splitting." Sanderlin was a leader in the integration of local schools and other institutions and later served as a circuit court judge. The *Times* observed that in St. Petersburg, the Eagle

Eye teams "deliberately attempted, by intimidation and delaying tactics, to discourage Negro voters—many of them using the franchise for the first time in their lives."

1968 ELECTION

In 1968, President Johnson withdrew his name for consideration for a second term due to his unpopularity over the Vietnam War and after a poor showing in the New Hampshire Primary. Vice President Hubert H. Humphrey then became the 1968 Democratic standard bearer. Humphrey's vice presidential running mate was Senator Edmund Muskie of Maine. Muskie spoke in St. Petersburg in October. The Republicans again nominated former vice president Richard Nixon. Nationally, the popular vote was close, with Nixon receiving 43.4 percent and Humphrey 42.7 percent. American Independent candidate Alabama governor George Wallace received the remaining 13.5 percent. Nixon received 56 percent of the electoral vote.

Nixon maintained the Republican presidential hold on Florida at the state level and crushed Humphrey in Pinellas with 50 percent of the vote versus Humphrey's 33 percent. Independent candidate and segregationist George Wallace garnered the remaining 16 percent. Democrats were virtually swept from local office, despite out-registering the Republicans by ten thousand votes. The lone survivor, in a close vote, was Clerk of the Court Pete Mullendore who served in that office from 1964 to 1981. Because of his repeated electoral success in what had become a Republican bastion, he earned the sobriquet of "Mr. Democrat."

In an editorial entitled "Straight Ticket Pinellas," the *Times* summed up the election by fuming, "Machine control in Pinellas is a reality, Straight-ticket voting has assured the hegemony of the Insco-Cramer-Young organization. It is...discouraging when the number of down-the-line Republican voters is so great that there is no distinction between the experienced legislator and the green newcomer....The challenge is clear, Democrats must begin to create the kind of progressive, appealing party that will be able to test the newly installed machine....Machine politics creates the forces that assure its destruction." The perceived "machine" even had the abbreviation "ICY." This referred to the three principals: Jack Insco, aide to Representative Cramer; Cramer himself; and then state senator (later congressman) C.W. Bill Young. Nevertheless, the *Times* praised the state for "keeping its cool" and not voting for Wallace, as did most of the Deep South.

1972 ELECTION

In 1972, Nixon repeated his win both nationally and in Florida and Pinellas, this time against Democratic South Dakota senator George McGovern. McGovern had two vice presidential candidates: Senator Thomas Eagleton of Missouri, who resigned after disclosure of a history of mental illness, and Sargent Shriver, who had served as ambassador to France and administrator for the Peace Corps and Head Start, the nationally funded preschool program. Eagleton had long made St. Petersburg his favorite vacation spot. After his resignation as the 1972 Democratic vice presidential candidate at McGovern's request, Eagleton was twice reelected to the Senate. Nixon had campaigned in St. Petersburg on behalf of state and congressional candidates in 1970 but did not make an appearance in 1972. His appearance in 1970 at the Bayfront Center before a crowd of seven thousand was the first time a sitting president had visited the city. One person not running in 1972 was Congressman Cramer. He had given up his House seat to run for the Senate two years earlier but lost to Democrat Lawton Chiles. Cramer was honored in 1974 by the Florida Republican State Executive Committee by being named "Mr. Republican" for his pioneer service in building the state Republican Party. In 2005, Interstate 275 was designated the "St. Petersburg Parkway/ William C. Cramer Memorial Parkway" in recognition of his efforts while in Congress to extend the interstate through St. Petersburg. The post office building on 1st Avenue North is also named in his honor.

Nixon won every state except Massachusetts. Nationally, he won 60.7 percent of the vote. He did even better in Pinellas with 69 percent of the vote. No Democrat won in Pinellas. The Republicans worked hard at getting out their vote and appealing for straight-ticket voting. Many Democrats split their ticket, especially for president. Nixon had a margin of over ninety thousand votes, while most local county-wide Republican candidates won by margins of about thirty thousand. Among the casualties was Bette Wimbish, St. Petersburg's first African American city councilperson, in a bid for the state Senate. She later served as Florida deputy secretary of commerce. St. Petersburg's black precincts voted mostly Democratic straight tickets. One exception was Republican school board candidate Martha Rudy Wallace, who garnered an exceptional number of African American votes.

1976 ELECTION

With Nixon's resignation over the Watergate Scandal in 1974, Vice President Gerald R. Ford of Michigan assumed the presidency. Ford was nominated as the Republican presidential candidate in 1976. His Democratic opponent was Jimmy Carter, governor of Georgia. President Ford visited St. Petersburg in February speaking to a predominantly elderly crowd at Williams Park. The size of the crowd was estimated at fifteen thousand people, a hard-to-believe number for such a small park. He said, "As long as I am President, we are going to keep the Social Security program and every other federal retirement program strong, sound, and certain." After the rally at Williams Park, he visited Bay Pines Veterans Hospital and pledged his support to replace the aging facility. Later in the year, Ford's son, Jack Ford, also made a brief appearance in St. Petersburg on behalf of his father, speaking to the Sertoma Club.

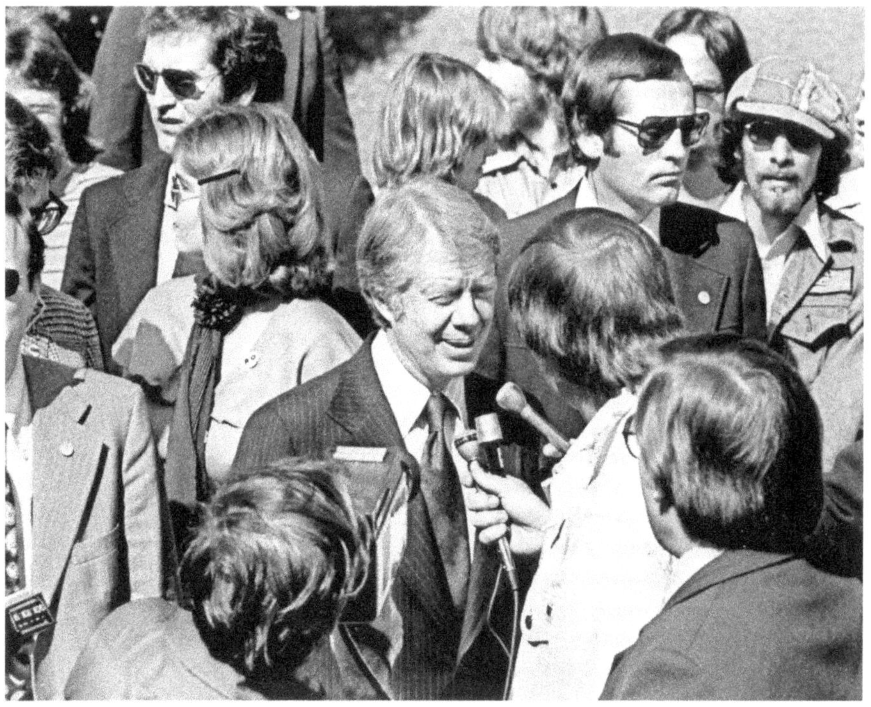

Jimmy Carter campaigning in St. Petersburg. Carter held a town hall meeting at the Historic Princess Martha Hotel, image 1980. *Courtesy St. Petersburg Museum of History.*

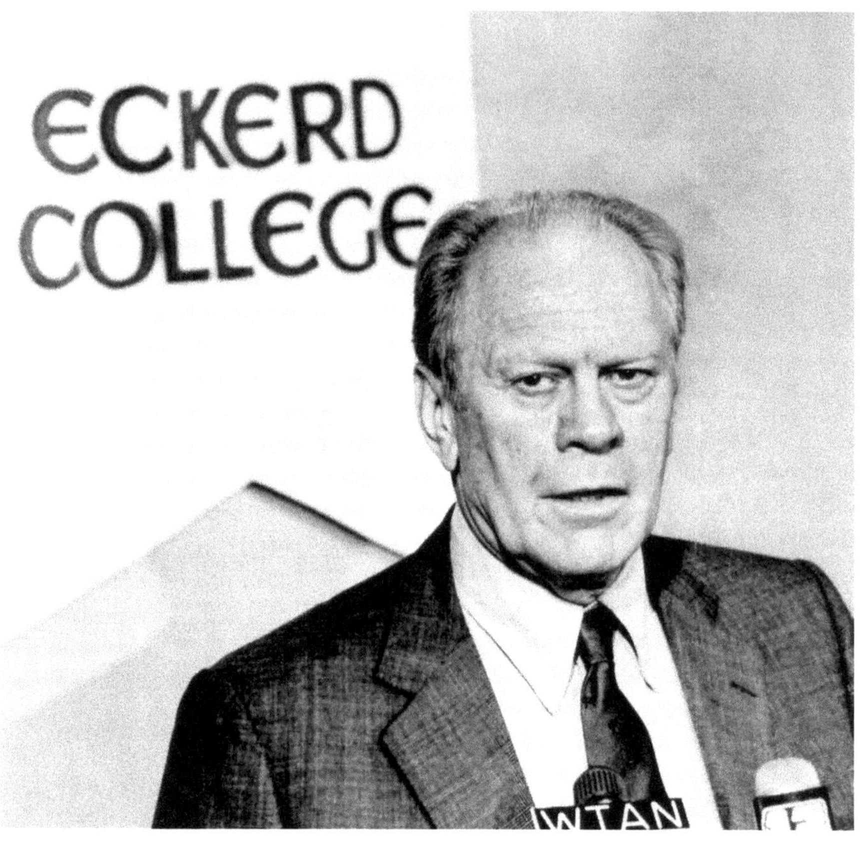

President Gerald Ford speaking at Eckerd College in 1983. Ford campaigned in St. Petersburg at Williams Park in 1976. *Courtesy St. Petersburg Museum of History.*

Carter won the national election with slightly more than 50 percent of the popular vote. However, Pinellas County continued its Republican tradition by voting for Ford, although the vote was close. But at the local level, Democrats swept most Republicans. Among the Democrats attaining office were teacher/union leader Don Chamberlain to the state Senate and St. Petersburg resident and former League of Women Voters president Jeanne Malchon to the County Commission. St. Petersburg Democratic city councilman Don Poindexter defeated Robert Melby to regain a St. Petersburg state House seat for the first time in twelve years. The *Times* welcomed the return of the two-party system to Pinellas.

1980 Election

The 1980 election pitted Californian Republican governor Ronald Reagan against incumbent Democratic president Jimmy Carter. Carter had lost popularity for a number of reasons, most prominent of which were the Iranian hostage crisis and the economy. Reagan's vice presidential running mate, George H.W. Bush, spoke at the Bayfront Concourse (now the Hilton) in September. He accused Carter's vice president, Walter Mondale, of "indulging in irresponsible, personalized attacks" on Governor Reagan. In October, President Carter visited St. Petersburg, where he held a town hall meeting at the Princess Martha Hotel. He pledged to protect Social Security and responded to concerns about inflation. After the town meeting, he made an unplanned visit to Bayfront Medical Center to visit a friend. Still later that month, Governor Reagan held a rally at Williams Park attended by 5,500. He received his greatest applause when he said, "A recession is when a neighbor loses his job. A depression is when you lose yours. A recovery will be when Jimmy Carter loses his." He also pledged to protect Social Security. As Reagan was about to speak, the bells at the nearby First Methodist Church began to peal. State Senator Henry Sayler, chairman of the State Republican Party, ran over to the church to curtail the concert.

Reagan won the national election in a landslide, with 50.7 percent of the vote to Carter's 41.0 percent. John B. Anderson of Illinois, a moderate Republican who ran as an independent, received 6.6 percent. Reagan did even better in Pinellas, and local Republicans were again returned to office. Reagan outpolled Carter by forty-seven thousand votes. Pinellas had become the most Republican county in the state. Of thirty-one elected offices, after the 1980 election Democrats held only three. Chamberlain and Malchon were voted out. However, of the twenty-eight candidates on the Republican ticket, seven were Democrats who joined the Republican Party just before they ran. Two referendum items of interest were also approved by voters. One was the countywide Emergency Medical Services (EMS) program. The other was the purchase of St. Petersburg gateway lands for parkland.

The 1980 vote in Pinellas was unusually slow. Results were not made known until six o'clock in the morning on Wednesday, to the frustration of many. The previous mechanical voting machines with levers had been replaced with a new punch-card system. Many ballots were folded, spindled, marked incorrectly and otherwise mutilated, confusing precinct workers as they sought to tally the votes. Some voters used a pencil or pen to mark the ballot rather than a stylus, and these had to be punched. (Hanging chads were not specifically mentioned!) Additionally, there was computer failure. Votes from forty precincts were accidentally deleted and had to be reentered. Supervisor of Elections Charles Kaniss stated, "Under the circumstances, the election ran just about as smooth as it could have. You know, when the newspapers don't have the results when they go home at 11 o'clock, they always think something's wrong." The 1980 vote was the largest yet—fifty-two thousand more than in the previous presidential election.

1984 Election

The 1984 election saw incumbent President Reagan run against former Democratic vice president Walter Mondale of Minnesota. Reagan's vice presidential running mate was again George H.W. Bush, and Mondale's running mate was Congresswoman Geraldine Ferraro of New York, the first woman to be nominated for vice president by a major party. In March, Bush campaigned at a rally in Williams Park, drawing a "crowd" of one thousand.

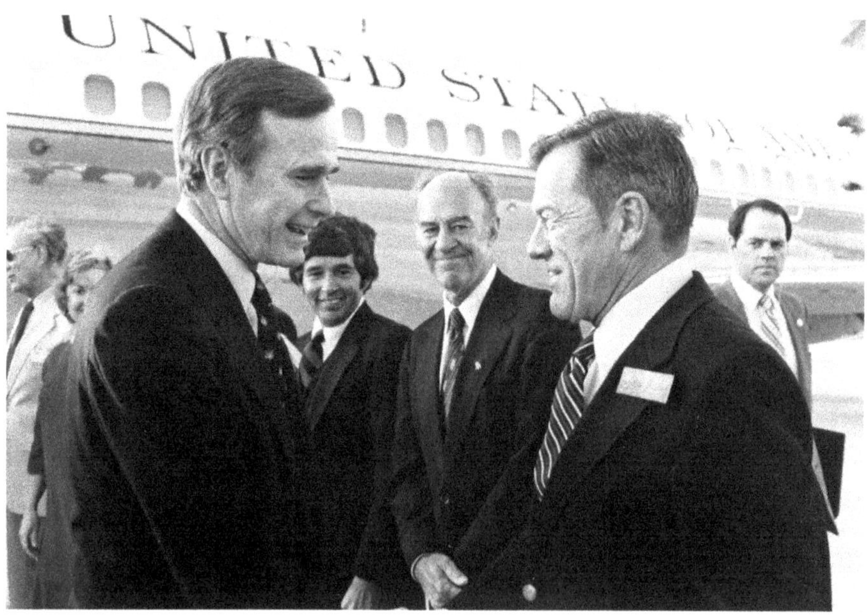

State Senator Henry Sayler greets Vice President (later President) George H.W. Bush. Businessman and philanthropist Jack Eckerd is in the background. Bush campaigned in St. Petersburg in both 1980 and 1984, image 1981. *Courtesy Sayler Family Collection.*

With the benefit of a strong economic recovery from the 1980–81 recession, Reagan swamped Mondale, winning 58.8 percent of the national popular vote and every state except Minnesota and the District of Columbia. Reagan beat Mondale in Pinellas with 65.0 percent of the vote. Pinellas Democrats began the election holding only six offices, four of which were up for reelection, and lost two of these. Survivors in the contested seats were State Representative Peter Rudy Wallace and property appraiser Ron Schultz. Losers were County Commissioner Gabe Cazares to George Greer and Patricia Bailey to Jim Frishe. Also on the ballot in St. Petersburg were charter amendments to provide for a property exchange, giving the city full title to the Vinoy fill; authorization of a seventy-four-slip marina in front of the Vinoy Hotel; and additional waterfront land to the charter protections, requiring a referendum for the sale or trade of city waterfront parkland. The first two of these amendments made possible the restoration of the historic Vinoy Hotel, helping to restart the downtown St. Petersburg economy. All were approved by large majorities.

SUMMARY AND ANALYSIS

Of the ten presidential elections between 1948 and 1984, the Republican presidential nominee won in Pinellas County and St. Petersburg in all but one. The sole exception was in 1964, when Lyndon Johnson carried the county with 55 percent of the vote. While it is difficult to tease out the reasons for a particular county voting for a president, some likely factors in the 1964 election were sympathy for the Democrats resulting from the assassination of President Kennedy only a year earlier and division within the Republican Party both at the national and local level. Much of this division centered on Goldwater's non-support of the 1964 Civil Rights Act. The differences in the candidates' positions over the Civil Rights Act appear to have significantly increased African American votes for Johnson, reversing Republican gains among African Americans that occurred in the 1956 election after the *Brown* school desegregation decision. President Ford's local win in 1976 was very close, and this was one of two elections in which Democrats made significant gains at the county level. Carter likely benefited from being a fresh face with southern roots, voters still upset over the Watergate scandal and Ford's pardon of former president Nixon. In neither of these cases do local issues appear to be a reason for Johnson's win or Carter's near win.

It also appears that in every election there was a presidential coattails effect at the county level. The best tests of this were the Johnson/Goldwater election in 1964 and the Carter/Ford election in 1976, both of which resulted in a significant number of Democrats winning offices previously held by Republicans at the local level.

In three of the ten elections between 1948 and 1984 (Truman/Dewey, Kennedy/Nixon and Carter/Ford), the national winner was different from the Pinellas winner. Prior to 1948, in two of eleven elections (Teddy Roosevelt/Parker and Taft/Bryan), the national winner was different from the Pinellas winner. In only two of these five Pinellas exceptional elections was the winner in Pinellas different from the winner in the state (Truman/Dewey and Carter/Ford). Between 1904 and 1984, St. Petersburg/Pinellas voted differently from the state as a whole on only four occasions (Harding, 1920; Coolidge, 1924; Dewey, 1948; and Ford, 1976). Overall, St. Petersburg/Pinellas reflected the state and national pattern during these periods.

Eisenhower's personal popularity as a war hero certainly helps explain his appeal in St. Petersburg and Pinellas County as a presidential candidate, but much of the success of the local Republican Party in the postwar period began in 1948 before his candidacy. To a certain extent, this represents the untiring efforts of people like Merle E. Rudy who reorganized a previously weak local Republican party, attended to registration, solicited visits by national Republican figures and got out the vote. It also had to do with the changing demographics of the times. The population of St. Petersburg had increased by 59 percent between 1940 and 1950, and another 87 percent between 1950 and 1960, and continued to grow (although more moderately) after that. As historian Arsenault noted, this in-migration was whiter and older and less southern. At the same time, the black population of the city had declined as a proportion, though continuing to grow in absolute numbers. Nevertheless, three Republican candidates won locally prior to 1948 (Harding, 1920; Coolidge, 1924; and Hoover, 1928, and Hoover almost won St. Petersburg again in 1932). This demonstrated the strong historic Republican roots in St. Petersburg and Pinellas County prior to the postwar boom, and these roots carried forth to influence the postwar elections.

Sources: Raymond Arsenault, *St. Petersburg and the Florida Dream: 1888–1950* (1988/1996); *St. Petersburg Times*, various dates; *Evening Independent*, various dates; Rick Baker, *Mangroves to Major League* (2000); Merle F. Rudy, manuscript on Pinellas Republican Party History, circa 1950; Pinellas County, *The Constitutional Officers of Pinellas County: A Brief History* (2006); Pinellas County Supervisor of Elections, various statistics; Florida Department of State, various statistics; Martha Rudy Wallace, "History of Pinellas County Republican Party," undated manuscript; and U.S. Census Bureau, various statistics.

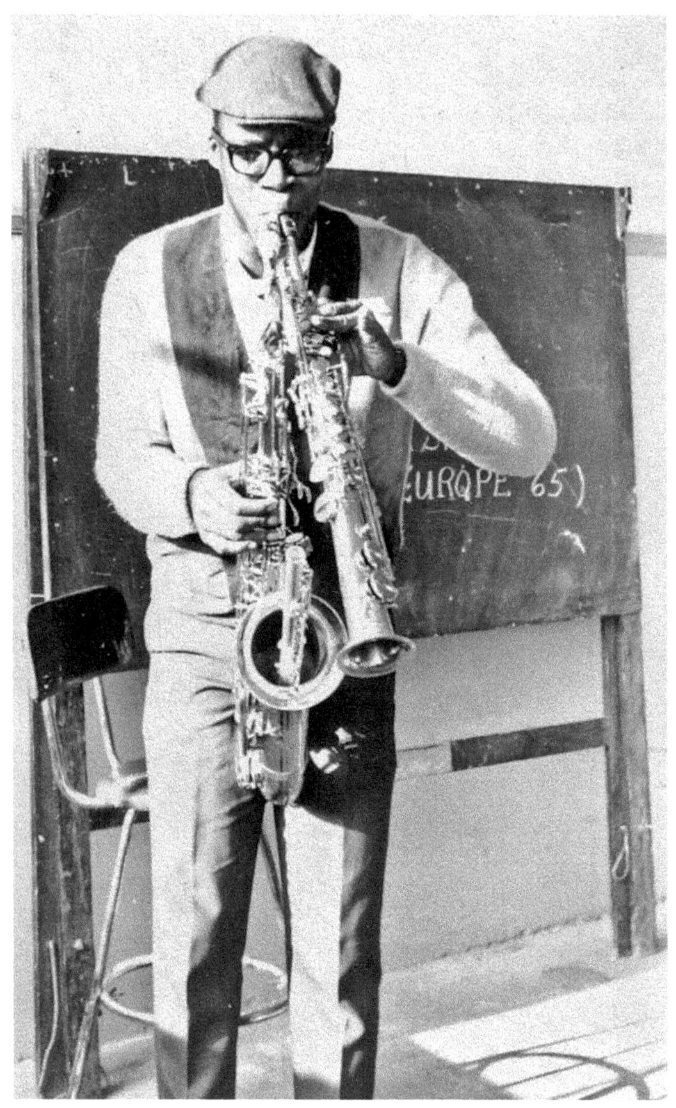

LeRoy L. Flemmings Jr. played tenor saxophone for James Brown, Otis Redding and Joe Tex, image circa 1964. *Courtesy LeRoy L. Flemmings Jr.*

Chapter 11

"James Brown Adopted Me"

LeRoy Flemmings Jr.

LeRoy L. Flemmings Jr. has a story to tell. As a youth in St. Petersburg, LeRoy and his best friend, Larry Davis, went every Saturday to Bringe's Music Store just to look at the shiny musical instruments in the display window. LeRoy dreamed about playing the trumpet and Larry the sax. At 16th Street Middle School, they kind of got their wish when they joined the school band—except LeRoy was given the sax to play and Larry the trumpet.

LeRoy had a passion for music. Much to his neighbors' displeasure, he practiced incessantly at his home in Jordan Park. He later played in the band at Gibbs High School under the guidance of "Prof" Reynolds Davis, the music director. LeRoy and Larry made the rounds of the African American Clubs just to hear the music—the Greenback Bank, the Manhattan Casino, High Stepper, Stud Club, Topper, Shangri-La and Roseland. But of greater importance, St. Petersburg was on the circuit of nationally known musical talent at the time—Ray Charles, B.B. King, Little Richard, Diana Washington, Dizzy Gillespie and more. LeRoy and Larry would follow these artists around offering to help unload equipment just to get to know them and their crews. LeRoy said that at the time "you could see the world if you got on the street."

He particularly remembered the Manhattan Casino. "It had a wooden floor. The building vibrated. Every artist that you could imagine came there. People were crushing against you. We were underage, fourteen or fifteen. To see those guys playing in their favorite clothes, just looking crazy....We would talk about how we were gonna do that. Every now and then the guys would come in the dressing room and they would talk to us about your skills and tell about all the great places they went and how many beautiful women there were, and all this madness you know. And I wanted to do this so badly."

While LeRoy was perfecting his skills on the sax, he also made acquaintance with Clayton Fillyau, who was involved in promoting musical programs in the Tampa Bay area and played drums with James Brown. Clayton was a pioneer in developing the "break beat" New Orleans drumming style. (Clayton was the brother of Ernest Fillyau, a photographer and member of the city council.) They hung out together and attended many musical programs. One day in 1963, Clayton tipped his friend LeRoy that James Brown needed a sax player. LeRoy immediately went to the booking offices where Brown was. There he found George Grogan, the booking agent for Universal Attractions, which arranged for most of the major African American shows in Florida. Grogan was also a chemistry teacher at Gibbs High School and a manager of Jordan Park public housing in what is now Midtown St. Pete. Grogan knew LeRoy well, as LeRoy lived in Jordan Park. "People were complaining about [my playing saxophone] all the time [at Jordan Park]." As LeRoy recalled, "When I got there [the booking offices], Mr. Grogan was sitting there. So I walked up. He wanted to know what I was doing there. 'Well, I heard James Brown needs a saxophone player.' I walked in the door." Grogan validated LeRoy's abilities for Brown, and he was hired on the spot. Not only that, but Brown told LeRoy the bus was leaving for the next stop in two hours and if he wanted the job he needed to be on it.

"I ran home. My mother was working. She worked six days a week and got Sunday off. She made thirty-five dollars a week. My aunt was home. I told her I got a job with James Brown at fifty dollars a night, but I needed five dollars, which she gave me. I took a shower and changed clothes and got a suitcase. I went downstairs and waited for my mother to come home. She did and asked me, 'Where are you going?' I told her. That was the beginning of my professional career."

JAMES BROWN

Flemmings continued:

> *James Brown adopted me. I was nineteen. He was the hottest artist out there. He was a strict guy for shoes being shined, creases on the trousers, bowtie on correctly. If you followed his rules, you were fine. If not, you got a $25 fine. I was making $350 a week. I never had a fine. The money that was fined went back to the band. Every five weeks or so, we would have a band picnic or banquet.*
>
> *It was nothing to work twenty or twenty-five days without a night off. Brown's style of music was completely original. Looking at it now I am amazed I was a part of that. There are just tremendous artists using a lot of his stuff. A lot of bands were copying his precision. Everything in that band was so air tight you couldn't put anything between it. There was no gap.*

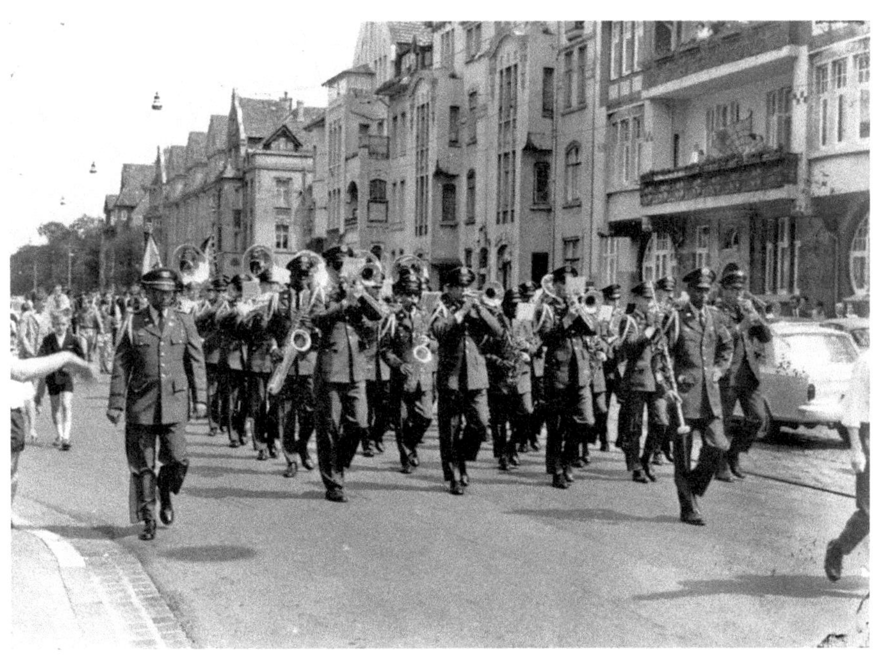

Flemmings also played with the 3rd Infantry Division Band in Europe. Here the band is performing in Hanover, Germany. Flemmings is first on the left in the second row, playing sax. "The musicians in the Army band were probably the best I played with in my whole life." Image 1965. *Courtesy LeRoy L. Flemmings Jr.*

> *We played for the queen of England when I was with James Brown—Buckingham Palace, costumes, guys with big hats. That's real. I got a chance to see that. The guys with the ruffles on. Abbey Hall, Big Ben, Trafalgar Square and those kinds of things. Just something you can't explain. You first have to do it. You read about it and see it on TV, but until you put your foot right on that spot, nobody can tell you what it's about. You have to do it yourself. We did Paris, France, Oxford, Manchester and Russell Square in London.*
>
> *James Brown said if you leave the band, you should have someone to replace you at least of your ability or better. I picked Maceo Parker. He became Brown's favorite team player.*

James Brown died in 2006 at the age of seventy-three. LeRoy was among the thousands who attended his memorial services.

3RD INFANTRY DIVISION BAND

Flemmings recalled:

> *I was with James Brown about two years. I went from James Brown to the army. I was drafted into the army in 1964. I was assigned to the 3rd Infantry Division Band in Wuerzburg, Germany. We were like the official army band for Europe, so whenever people like President Johnson came through, or Alexander Haig, we were the persons that played for them. The musicians in the Army band were probably the best I played with in my whole life. There were seventy-four guys—top-flight musicians. But the pay got to me—ninety-nine dollars a month. I was in the army one year, eleven months and twenty-three days. The structure was good for me. Gave me a sense of teamwork.*
>
> *I personally believe that every guy needs to go into the army, or some sort of military service, for the discipline if nothing else. Plus it affords a chance to see things that otherwise you would not see. That's my personal opinion.*
>
> *After leaving the army, I came back to St. Pete for a week—ten days—and got a job with a guy named Otis Redding. Two months later, I was back in Europe. This was Redding's first trip ever to Europe as an entertainer. I had a chance to see the guys I had just left in the army. They asked "how are things in the world." That meant in civilian life.*

Otis Redding's style was country. He was a plain guy, a farmer basically. He came from Georgia. He was a very impetuous kind of fellow. He played the guitar, called a "Hit Maker," did his own tuning. He was someone you could play with and relax. He was not as high strung as James Brown. James Brown was so rigid.

LeRoy remembered Redding leaving him and the rest of the band stranded in a London hotel. Redding left without paying them. They had to sneak out of the hotel without paying. They got to Heathrow Airport only to be fogged in, expecting the Bobbies to arrive at any moment. The fog lifted, they boarded the plane and returned to New York. Eventually, Redding did pay them. LeRoy was with Redding for just a few months. But in that short time, he participated in the recording of three of Redding's hit singles: "Fa-Fa-Fa-Fa-Fa," "Try a Little Tenderness" and "(Sittin' On) The Dock of the Bay." The latter hit was issued after Redding's shocking death. The Rock and Roll Hall of Fame includes "Tenderness" and "Dock" as two of five hundred songs that shaped rock-and-roll.

Redding's career was tragically ended in a plane crash in December 1967. He was only twenty-six. LeRoy had left Redding a few months before. One of the reasons he left was because of the plane Redding had bought to transport his band. LeRoy did not like the looks of it and immediately decided he would not fly on it. The cause of the crash was never exactly determined.

JOE TEX

At the time he heard of Redding's death, LeRoy was performing with Joe Tex, the soul singer and songwriter. In addition to LeRoy, there were six other musicians on stage who had played with Redding. The entire band stopped their performance and got down on their knees and prayed. LeRoy played with Joe Tex until 1968. During his time with Tex, he performed in Hawaii, Japan and Australia. One of Tex's hits during this period was "Skinny Legs and All" (1967). Another signature hit was "Hold What You've Got" (1965). Both sold more than 1 million copies. He was awarded a Gold Disc by the Recording Industry Association of America (RIAA) in 1968 and again in 1972. A feud developed between Joe Tex and James Brown. Tex accused Brown of copying his stage moves. Brown began dating Tex's wife.

On one occasion, Tex mocked Brown's closing routine of throwing a cape over his shoulder and shouted, "Please—get me out of this cape!" Brown later fired a gun at Tex in a nightclub.

GROWING UP IN ST. PETE

LeRoy recalled growing up in St. Pete. His stepfather, Levi Daniels, was the first black butcher at Webb's City to sell meat directly to customers.

> *While the '50s and '60s were not good in St. Pete, it wasn't as bad as it could have been—not as bad as Mississippi or Alabama. But there were just places you didn't go. We went fishing at Demens Landing. It used to be called "the Bay." That's also where we went swimming. We couldn't go to Spa Beach. You could fish at the Pier, but you couldn't swim there.*
>
> *You could fish on the west side of Lake Maggiore. But you would never be caught there after dark. It was just a rule. Blacks at that time could not be on the south side of 15th Avenue South unless you were working or had business there. I participated in the sit-ins at McCrory's and Kress's lunch counters. There was a white woman with us as part of a picket line. She was hit in the head with a board. At that time, the ambulance service was provided by funeral homes. An ambulance from a white funeral home arrived and refused to drive her to the hospital. She had to wait for an ambulance from a black funeral home. This was crazy. Black baseball players could not stay in hotels. They had to stay in the black community or the Robert James Hotel* [owned by black dentist Robert James Swain]*; otherwise they slept on a bus. But St. Petersburg was not really a bad place; it really wasn't. It was not as bad as Mississippi, Alabama. One time a guy told me, "I spent a whole year in Alabama one day." I saw a guy hanging from a tree in Mississippi in '63 along Interstate 10. I will never forget that.*
>
> *Musicians have had to come home because we all play together. We have a jam session over there—black and white. Musicians somehow or another, people who are artists, tend to get through those kind of issues. We know what we were. I'm black. He knows he's white. But the music doesn't have any color. When you're playing, all the notes are the same.*

Coming Home

After his time with James Brown, the 3rd Infantry Division Band, Otis Redding and Joe Tex, LeRoy Flemmings relocated to Los Angeles for a time. While there, the smog injured his throat so that he had to stop playing the sax. He took up the base and played that for many years. In 1990, he again began to play the tenor sax. He eventually returned to St. Petersburg and got his master's degree at the University of South Florida in music education with a minor in performance saxophone. He then started a teaching career as band director at Horace Mann Jr. High in Brandon. He later returned to his alma mater, Gibbs High School in St. Petersburg, and also taught at Lakewood High School, as well as at several elementary schools, again holding the position of band director. He also had his own local band and would play with such musicians as Al Downing and Ernie Calhoun. In 1996, he retired from teaching. For many years, he volunteered in the Jazz Studies Program at Boca Ciega High School with Frank Williams. Frank said, "LeRoy is one of my heroes. He has the distinction of being the only person who was Band Director at two high schools at the same time, Gibbs and Lakewood. He is a great musician. He is great with kids and loves what he does." LeRoy has his own band, Time Changers, and additionally plays in the Phil Hill Trio. LeRoy lives in Midtown and is a member of Mount Zion AME Church.

Early James Brown Hits

1959 "Try Me"
1960 "Think"
1961 "Bewildered"
1962 "Night Train"
1963 "Prisoner of Love"
1964 "Out of Sight"
1964 "Please, Please, Please"*
1965 "Papa's Got a Brand New Bag"*
1966 "It's a Man's Man's Man's World"*
1967 "Bring It Up"

Otis Redding Single Hits

1962 "These Arms Are Mine"*
1964 "Mr. Pitiful"*
1964 "Stand by Me"

1965 "I've Been Loving You Too Long"
1965 "Just One More Day"*
1965 "Respect"*
1965 "That's How Strong My Love Is"*
1965 "I Can't Turn You Loose"*
1966 "(I Can't Get No) Satisfaction"*
1966 "My Lover's Prayer"*
1966 "Fa-Fa-Fa-Fa-Fa (Sad Song)"*
1967 "Shake"*
1967 "Glory of Love"*
1967 "Try A Little Tenderness"*
1967 "Knock on Wood"
1967 "Tramp"*@
1968 "(Sittin' On) The Dock of the Bay"*@#
1968 "The Happy Song (Dum-Dum)"*
1968 "I've Got Dreams to Remember"*
1968 "Merry Christmas, Baby"#
1968 "Papa's Got A Brand New Bag"* (new version of James Brown's original)
1969 "A Lover's Question"*
1969 "Love Man"*

JOE TEX SINGLE HITS

1965 "Hold What You Got"#
1966 "A Sweet Woman Like You"*
1966 "S.Y.L.J.F.M. (The Letter Song)"
1966 "I Believe I'm Gonna Make It"
1966 "I've Got to Do a Little Bit Better"
1966 "Papa Was Too"
1967 "Show Me"
1967 "Skinney Legs and All"
1968 "Chicken Crazy/Buying a Book"
1968 "I'll Never Do You Wrong/Wooden Spoon"
1968 "Keep the One You Got/Go Home and Do It"
1968 "Men Are Getting Scarce/You Gonna Thank Me, Woman"
1972 "I Gotcha"*#
1972 "Cat's Got Her Tongue/Woman Stealer"
1976 "Have You Ever"
1976 "Love Shortage"

1977 "Ain't Gonna Bump No More"@#
1979 "Loose Caboose"

Notes: *rhythm and blues hit; @U.K. hit; #U.S. hit

Sources: *St. Petersburg Times*, especially January 27, 1964; and conversations with LeRoy Flemmings Jr., Frank Williams and Ernest Calhoun.

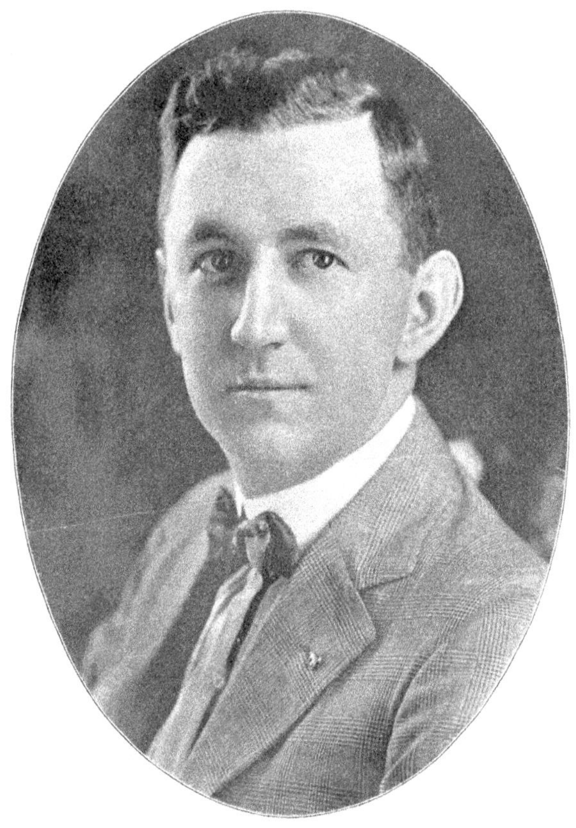

Aymer Vinoy Laughner (1883–1961) built the Vinoy Park Hotel. Laughner was from Pennsylvania, where he and his father made their fortunes in the oil business. *Courtesy the Renaissance Vinoy Resort.*

Chapter 12

THE VINOY LEGACY

The historic Vinoy Park Hotel was built by Aymer Vinoy Laughner in 1925. The architect was Henry Taylor, who also designed St. Mary's Church, Comfort Station No. 1, the Jungle Hotel (now Admiral Farragut), the Jungle Prado nightclub/shopping center and the Florida Theater. The Vinoy's contractor was George Miller, who also built the nearby Soreno Hotel, the Belleview Biltmore Hotel and Tampa's Citrus Exchange. Cost of constructing the Vinoy was $3.5 million, at the time the largest construction project in Florida history. The Vinoy was the largest and most luxurious of St. Petersburg's boom-era hotels.

According to historic hotel author Prudy Taylor Board, the Vinoy was sparked as the result of a wager made between Laughner and 1920s golf champion Walter Hagen. At a party at Laughner's house on Beach Drive near the present site of the Vinoy, Laughner bet Hagen that he could not hit golf balls off the top of Laughner's watch without breaking the crystal. Hagen won the wager. When Laughner and another guest went to retrieve the balls from the neighbor's lawn, the guest commented on what a nice site the waterfront home would be for a hotel. The rest was hotel history.

Aymer's father was Perry O. Laughner. Perry made his fortune in Pennsylvania oil and then relocated to St. Petersburg in 1919. After arriving in the city, father and son founded a development company that bought more than two thousand acres in St. Petersburg and other areas of Pinellas County. Laughner Enterprises Inc. owned the West Coast Inn near St. Pete's Waterfront Park baseball field, much of Beach Drive and a piece of real estate on Central Avenue. Aymer was named after a dashing hero of a nineteenth-century novel.

The Vinoy Park Hotel came to be famous for its gourmet cuisine and celebrity guests. These did not always go together. An early visitor was former president Calvin Coolidge, known for his simple tastes. According to hotel lore, he preferred to eat in the employees' cafeteria rather than in the hotel's fine restaurant. Other early hotel guests of note included former president Herbert Hoover, explorer Admiral Richard Byrd, novelist Ernest Hemingway, essayist H.L. Mencken and actor Jimmy Stewart, to name a few. It has not been documented that baseball legend Babe Ruth actually stayed at the hotel, but he spent a lot of time there and was a good friend of the Laughner family. The film *The Break*, with Vince Van Patten, was filmed at the Vinoy in 1995.

The Vinoy continued as a luxury seasonal hotel until World War II. The season ran from December to early April—there was no air conditioning. During the war years, guests stopped coming, and the hotel was converted into housing for the army air corps and, later, as an R&R facility for the U.S. Maritime Commission. After the war, the hotel struggled. In 1945, Laughner sold the Vinoy to Alsonett Hotels, a hotel chain based in Chicago owned by Charles Alberding. Alberding at first succeeded in again making the hotel a success but eventually found it a losing proposition. In 1972, Bob Reynolds, only twenty years old at the time, offered to buy the hotel from Alberding. Bob was a St. Petersburg native who had fallen in love with the hotel as a child and always harbored an ambition to own it. Surprisingly, Alberding agreed to sell it even though Reynolds only had $10,000 cash. A lease was drawn up with a six-month option to purchase the hotel for $5 million. Reynolds organized as R.W. Enterprises with four partners. Reynolds then enlisted architect and soon-to-be city mayor C. Randolph (Randy) Wedding to draw up plans for the hotel's restoration. Wedding also soon became treasurer and a major advocate for the project. But Reynolds and Wedding failed to obtain the necessary financial backing. In 1974, for the first time in its history, the hotel was closed. In late 1975, the hotel was reopened. In an act of desperation, rates were slashed from $50 a night to a mere $7. The once elegant ballroom was used for public dances, card parties and even volleyball. But even these radical changes failed to keep the hotel afloat and soon even the Vinoy's remaining fine furnishings were sold to help pay bills. The Vinoy was again closed in 1975. It was not just the Vinoy that was in bad shape in the 1980s but rather the entire downtown. The commercial wind had been sucked out of the downtown area with the

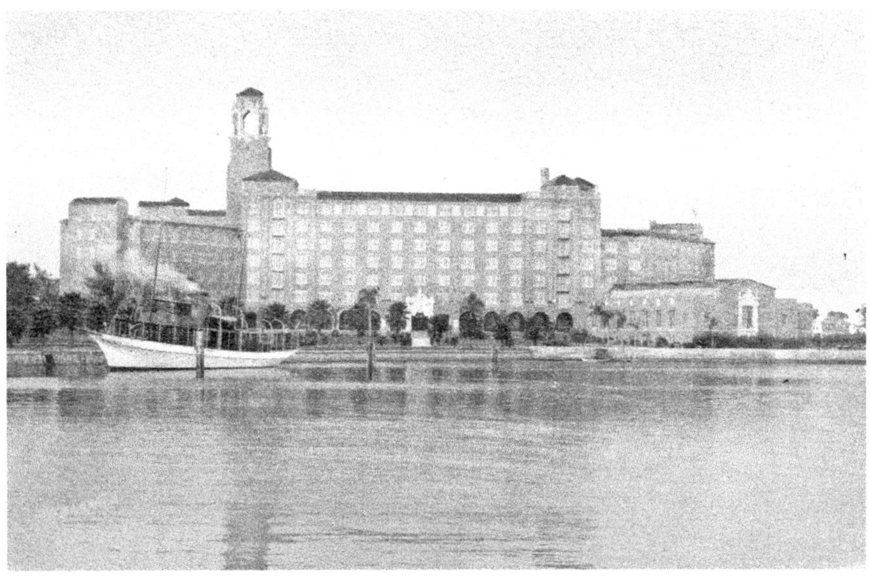

The Vinoy Park Hotel at its pre–World War II zenith. This highly collectable hand-colored postcard was published by noted photographer E.G. Barnhill. The Vinoy later published copies. *Courtesy Michaels Family Collection.*

opening of Central Plaza on Highway 19, the rise of suburban shopping in the 1950s and the construction of Tyrone Mall in 1972. The last major downtown retail store, Maas Brothers, closed in 1991.

In 1978, the Vinoy was named to the National Register of Historic Places, making it possible for investors to obtain federal tax breaks. Craig McLaughlin, who was later a principal in the Vinoy's restoration, recalled that the project eventually received federal tax credits amounting to 25 percent of the project's hard costs. In 1986, it was also designated a local landmark. Still later it was added to the National Trust for Historic Preservation's Historic Hotels of America.

The hotel was to languish for the next seventeen years. Horror stories abounded. One journalist wrote, "The hotel brings to mind Blanche DuBois, the faded beauty from *A Streetcar Named Desire*. She always depended on the kindness of strangers, who often did her wrong." He went on, "This lady is a mess….Pigeons fly into the grand ballroom as vines crawl through the windows." On one city-led tour in the late 1980s, potential developers walked in to find a nonpaying guest roasting one of the pigeons on a stick over a small fire he had started in the lobby. Standing water was a breeding ground for mosquitos. High school kids sneaked in to drink beer and play kickball in the ruins of the main dining room. At one point, the hotel was fenced in and patrolled by guard dogs, but the dogs got loose and ran about the waterfront. Celebrated *Times* columnist Jeff Klinkenberg reported rumors of "at least one hungry alligator [in the basement] with an appetite for rodents and misplaced feet."

In 1980, Alberding refused to renew the lease with R.W. Enterprises and let new leases in succession to Gulfport developer Arthur H. Padula, St. Petersburg businessman Robert V. Workman and then Jerome J. Palumbo of Cincinnati. In 1983, Craig McLaughlin and B.B. Anderson of the B.B. Anderson Development Co. of Kansas bought the lease from Palumbo. McLaughlin and Anderson teamed up with L. Bert Stephens, a former associate of Alberding and a hotel operator. Stephens enlisted the participation of Fred Guest, a well-respected retired stockbroker, investor and investment banker from New York. Guest had been interested in buying the Boca Raton Resort hotel that Stephens operated. When that deal fell through, Stephens told Guest about the Vinoy. Guest came to see the hotel and, as he later reported, "immediately fell in love with it" despite its deplorable condition. Fred Guest became the principal advocate for the project. They formed a partnership and began what some derided as "Fred's Folly." At the time, hotels were particularly difficult properties to finance. The fact that it was also a historic hotel, while offering potential tax and marketing advantages, added to the difficulty because of the special approvals required for construction.

The partnership determined that in order to make the Vinoy a success, it needed boat slips in the North Yacht Basin and city-owned land adjacent to Seventh Avenue for tennis courts, including most of Baywood Park. Baywood Park was a small park that included a shallow Indian mound adjacent to the Vinoy. Baywood was commonly considered at the time to be part of the waterfront parks receiving special protection in the City Charter. This included the need for a public referendum on any sale or long-term lease of waterfront parkland. In its zeal to accommodate the Vinoy development, the city council contemplated an ordinance that would effectively redefine Baywood as *not* a waterfront park and avoid a referendum. Preservationists and others protective of the Waterfront Parks, led by former mayor Charles Schuh, attorney Peter Belmont and others, immediately called foul and challenged the city's decision in court. After Circuit Judge Mark McGarry ruled that Baywood was indeed a waterfront park, the council backed down and agreed to a compromise. A referendum would be held proposing the exchange of most of Baywood Park and some other adjacent city land, and the submerged land in front of the Vinoy, for a little over six acres of land owned by the Vinoy that is now essentially Vinoy Park. The land to be ceded to the Vinoy was restricted to recreational use. But the referendum also included stronger provisions in the City Charter clearly defining the waterfront parks. As part of a related out-of-court settlement, the city also agreed to enact a local preservation ordinance, which was accomplished in 1986. The Vinoy was among the first buildings to be designated local landmarks under the ordinance.

A referendum on the swap was scheduled for 1984. Shortly before the required referendum was to be held, the partnership held an open house. An estimated ten thousand people turned out, demonstrating both curiosity and the deep emotional attachment many had for the Vinoy. The referendum received overwhelming approval. In 1986, Guest, McLaughlin and Stephens organized as the Vinoy Development Corporation and worked out another lease with Alberding. In 1988, the corporation enlisted the help of Smith Barney investment bankers to find an equity player to invest in the hotel and manage it. An agreement was secured with Stouffer Hotels and Resorts.

The 1984 referendum included a provision that the boat slips had to be built within four years. Despite Guest and company's many efforts, they were not able to obtain financing within that period, and another referendum was held in 1989 to sustain the earlier decision. The *St. Petersburg Times* had supported the 1984 proposal but opposed the matter the second time, arguing that the boat slips could be added later after the developers obtained financing. The developers argued the reverse, saying that the marina approval was necessary to obtain the financing. The 1989 referendum was also approved, this time by a close vote.

Financing was soon obtained, and restoration construction began in earnest. The developers and architect were fervent in seeking to restore the hotel to its original historic design. They sought to install new wiring, plumbing and air conditioning in a manner that minimally infringed on the original décor. Local artist Tom Stovall and his two-man crew worked eight hours a day for three months restoring by hand the friezes, borders and panels of just the dining room. Much of the work was done lying on their backs. The staff architect for the state Bureau of Historic Preservation closely followed the restoration. After it was completed, he said, "I've seldom been involved with a project that has spent this much time to restore the old materials, old designs and finishes." In addition to the restoration of the original hotel, a parking garage and 105-room tower were also constructed.

The developers further acquired the Sunset Golf course on Snell Isle to become a part of the hotel's amenities, and famed golf course architect Ron Garl was enlisted to renovate the course. The Women's Tennis Association was also convinced to make the new Vinoy its headquarters.

The hotel was officially reopened on July 31, 1992. Total restoration costs amounted to $93 million (approximately $158 million in today's dollars). That was 58 percent more than the cost of constructing the Barnett Tower (now Priatek Plaza), the city's tallest office building. The hotel restoration was originally packaged with construction of condominiums to be located just east of the hotel. However, this did not materialize until long after the restoration was completed. In 2000, after still another referendum, the Vinoy added the $10 million Palm Court Ballroom (convention center). In 1996, the Vinoy was purchased by the Renaissance Hotel Group, headquartered in Hong Kong. Walton Street Capital of Chicago then acquired the hotel in 2005. It is now the property of FelCor Lodging Trust of Dallas but is still managed by Marriott. Since restoration, the hotel's guests have included such notables as President Jimmy Carter and wife Rosalynn; President George H.W. Bush and wife Barbara; Vice President Al Gore; Vice President Joe Biden; Governor Mitt Romney and wife Ann; U.S. House Speaker Paul Ryan; Condoleezza Rice; actors Robin Williams, Susan Sarandon, Martin Sheen, Jon Voight and Omar Sharif; singer Frankie Avalon; and General Norman Schwarzkopf, to name a few.

The current era of downtown revitalization may be divided into four phases: 1) The Events Prior to 1999, most notably the restoration of the Vinoy Hotel; 2) The First Wave of Downtown Condos; 3) The Second Wave of Downtown Condos; and 4) The Post-Recession Period.

PHASE 1: THE VINOY RESTORATION ERA

The restoration of the Vinoy is credited by many with being a major catalyst for downtown revitalization, particularly near the waterfront. Fred Guest envisioned it that way. Long before the restoration was accomplished, he said, "There have certainly been a lot of skeptics about downtown St. Petersburg. But we're true believers in where St. Pete is going. I've felt for years that this was a town just waiting to happen, and I think in a couple of years this is going to be a spectacular city." In a 1992 statement, he said, "There was a special window—1986, '87–'88...the Dome [Tropicana Field stadium] was under way, Bay Plaza, the Mahaffey Theater, The Pier—it was before the recession, when it looked as if a lot of things were coming together for the city....Now many are looking to the Vinoy as the psychological boost that will make the long-hoped for downtown rejuvenation a reality." Guest spoke of the "intertwined future of the hotel and the city" and said he hoped that "the hotel can generate spinoff success: restaurants and retail, even relocations by executives who stay at the hotel and find the city a good place to do business." Later, in a 2012 *Times* interview, he said, "I believed St. Pete could be this beautiful city, which it is now, and that the hotel would be the heart of it and people locally would join and other people would come from other parts of the world to visit."

The restoration itself removed an eyesore from one of the downtown's most prominent locations. A derelict Vinoy cut short any interest investors might have had in the city. The hotel is an important economic engine for the city's economy in its own right, now employing about five hundred people and generating annual revenue of nearly $50 million and various taxes totaling nearly $6 million. But more importantly, the Vinoy's reopening eventually played a major role in stimulating new construction and business, especially along Beach Drive and other nearby areas; helped make new financing available for additional development projects; and had an important psychological effect on investor confidence. As architect and Cloisters developer Randy Wedding said, "There was a lot of back pressure built up for a long period of time. The problem was that people were a bit timid about it [investing]."

Interpreting the cold statistical data available from the city on major construction throughout the downtown between 1985 and 2010 is challenging. If one were to graph it and control for inflation, there would be no steady progression of construction dating from the Vinoy. Prior to the Vinoy restoration in 1992, there were significant developments in 1985 (South Trust Tower), 1987 (Hilton Hotel Renovation), 1988 (Mahaffey Renovation), 1990 (Tropicana Field) and 1991 (Barnett Tower). Two of these, the Mahaffey and Tropicana Field, were largely publicly funded projects. While Tropicana was not completed until 1990, the city first committed funding for it in 1983. Subsequent to the Vinoy restoration there were also significant medical construction projects in 1994 and 1995 (Suncoast Medical, Bayfront and All Children's) and in 1997 another significant public investment in getting the Trop ready for baseball.

Martin Normile, formerly president of St. Petersburg Progress, was a close observer of the Vinoy's restoration and downtown's revitalization. He stated:

> *Not to diminish the real and symbolic significance of the Vinoy as a catalyst to downtown's continuing development (even today), but St. Petersburg's 1980s push for major-league baseball and the stadium set the stage to attract the developer's attention and investment in the Vinoy. The very controversial stadium decision demonstrated St. Petersburg's determination and commitment to downtown redevelopment. Fred Guest and others saw in the stadium decision that St. Petersburg was serious and well organized about pushing forward with development. If the city, county and business community was so willing to take on that kind of project, then something special was about to happen in downtown. It provided credibility and momentum.*

Guest's partner and president of the Vinoy Development Corporation, Craig McLaughlin, said, "The building of the stadium was huge for the Vinoy—sleepy old St. Pete rolling dice on a baseball stadium without a team. That was an image changer. Was it genius or was it folly?" Guest and McLaughlin thought it was genius. Similarly, Dave Fischer, mayor at the time the Vinoy opened and when St. Petersburg obtained a baseball franchise, stated, "One thing baseball did early for us was stimulating the imagination of those who developed the hotel."

While the stadium helped get attention of investors in the Vinoy and other projects to follow, McLaughlin saw the opening of the Florida International Museum as of greater immediate importance with respect to downtown's revitalization. The museum was heavily subsidized by philanthropist John W. Galbraith and the city. It opened in 1995 with the Treasures of the Czars exhibit in the former Maas Brothers Department Store. The exhibit drew an amazing 600,000 visitors, more than twice the population of the city.

Former mayor David Fischer was instrumental in obtaining the Czars exhibit. Originally, the plan was to bring an exhibit on Catherine the Great. Mayor Fischer and former St. Petersburg College president Carl Kuttler flew to St. Petersburg, Russia, to make arrangements. Upon arrival, they were escorted for three or four days by none other than Vladimir Putin, who at that time was an assistant to the city mayor. After the visit to St. Petersburg, Fischer made a side trip to Moscow. While there, he visited the Kremlin museums, which held the treasures of the czars. Later, when negotiations for the Catherine exhibit fell through, he managed to secure the treasures of the czars, which had never before left the country.

The Czars exhibit was topped in 1997–98 by the *Titanic* exhibit, drawing 800,000 visitors. By comparison, the city's most popular museum, the Dalí, was on track in 2014 to reach a record 400,000 visitors. The International Museum continued to operate until 2007; however, later exhibits were far less successful than Czars and *Titanic*. Nevertheless, the museum had a significant impact on the downtown. Stores and restaurants sprang up near the museum almost overnight. A 1996 *Times* article hyping the Alexander the Great exhibit listed forty-five restaurants and cafés within walking distance of the museum. A similar list printed in 1998 for the Empires of Mystery exhibit had grown to sixty-four. Restaurants would even coordinate their menus to fit exhibit themes. Mel Sembler, developer of nearby BayWalk (now the Sundial), stated that he never would have launched the shopping and entertainment complex if it hadn't been for the museum. An economic impact study estimated that the Czars exhibit alone generated $34 million outside the museum. The exhibit's impact even rippled over to the Fine Arts Museum and Pier, helping break visitation records there.

According to McLaughlin, the International Museum was significant in indirectly attracting new residents downtown. He also credited the "Get Downtown First Friday" events that date from the time of the International Museum and still continue. Prospective residents demanded restaurants and night life, and the museum stimulated that. They also demanded shopping, and BayWalk helped to provide that. Later, in 2003, the downtown Publix and CVS pharmacy were added. "It also gave the Vinoy something to market," said McLaughlin. "Guests came to the Vinoy to see the Treasures of the Czars and later *Titanic*. The Vinoy's guests liked what they saw in St. Pete. They especially appreciated the downtown Waterfront Parks and the proximity to the bay. Some decided to make St. Pete their home and influenced their friends to move to St. Pete as well." The Vinoy, the museum and the restaurants and retail again "created life" in the downtown, he added.

PHASE 2: FIRST WAVE OF DOWNTOWN CONDOS

None of the development to occur during this first phase was on Beach Drive or immediately adjacent to it. None of it was residential. Then, in 1999, a second phase of revitalization began when a wave of residential condos began hitting the waterfront starting with the Cloisters, soon followed by the Florencia, Vinoy Place and the Madison apartments, two blocks west of the Mahaffey. McLaughlin views this second phase as finally giving the downtown a "residential address." These developments led the way in again validating downtown as a desirable place to live.

After the 1992 reopening of the Vinoy, it took time to successfully reposition the hotel in the hospitality industry. Additionally, the nation was just coming out of a recession, and lodging revenue actually did not regain 1990 levels until 1996. The recession also put a damper on lending. New projects require lead time before construction begins. Planning and securing financing for a project to break ground in 1997 might typically start two or three years earlier. Taking that into consideration, given the reopening of the Vinoy in July 1992, the Vinoy's impact was fairly quick. Ground was broken for the Cloisters in 1997, with opening in 1999. The lead architect for the Cloisters was Randy Wedding, previously a major player in R.W. Enterprises' bid to restore the Vinoy. Ground was broken for the Vinoy Place condos in 1998, three years before completion in 2001.

Jack Bowman, longtime St. Petersburg realtor and one of the developers of the Cloisters, said in a 2012 statement, "The Vinoy was the first piece of the puzzle. Guest took the chance, and he gets the credit. He saw there was something here worth doing. If it hadn't been for him, we probably wouldn't have done what we did." Bob Ulrich, also a partner in the Cloisters, was mayor when Guest started the Vinoy venture. "The impact [of the Vinoy] was huge. It's impossible to measure the amount of influence it had on further development," he noted. "There's no other project downtown with the exception of the Dome [Tropicana Field] that anybody has put $95 million into. I do know there were other projects that lenders were reluctant to fund without the Vinoy. We might have had a difficult time financing [the Cloisters] without the Vinoy."

Mike Cheezem, CEO of JMC Communities, said in a 2002 interview that the Vinoy opened the way for the Florencia on Beach Drive. "It was a real big factor in our decision to build that community, the Vinoy's stature, its success, the quality of what they did, the clientele they were attracting." The Florencia broke ground in 1998 and was completed in 2000. In the same interview, Mayor Rick Baker summed it up: "I have always felt that bringing back downtown was a three-legged stool: Getting the Vinoy renovated, bringing baseball downtown, and getting an entertainment center into downtown. The Vinoy really kicked off the renovation of downtown St. Petersburg."

PHASE 3: THE SECOND WAVE OF DOWNTOWN CONDOS

McLaughlin saw these first Beach Drive projects as a test of the market. Could three downtown condos built at about the same time be successful? Had the downtown again achieved the "synergy" and "critical mass" necessary for sustained development? The answer was a resounding "yes." Once that was clear, the third phase of downtown revitalization began five years later. Starting in 2006 and continuing into 2009 was another wave of construction that included Parkshore Plaza, 1010 Central, the Sage, 400 Beach, Ovation and Signature Place. There was also significant construction at USF and Mahaffey. Then building again paused as the effects of the Great Recession of 2008–9 set in. But while the building market paused, McLaughlin's perception was that the demand for living in downtown St. Pete did not. For example, he believed that despite the recession the downtown area saw yet another record number of restaurants.

PHASE 4: THE POST-RECESSION PERIOD

We are now in a fourth phase, with development reaching yet another peak. In 2010, All Children's opened a new hospital. The new Dalí Museum opened in 2011, as did Fusion Apartments on Central. St. Anthony's Hospital underwent a major expansion in 2012. The Historic Birchwood Inn opened on Beach Drive in 2014. Within a mile of the downtown Waterfront Parks, thirteen additional projects have either been recently completed or are underway. Seven of these are apartment buildings rather than condos, reflecting a new trend. One development, to be built on the long near-vacant Tropicana Block on Central Avenue, combines a thirteen-story hotel as part of a forty-one-story condo tower. The condo tower will be taller than the city's current tallest building, Priatek Plaza. The owners of Priatek Plaza, Kucera Properties, plan an $85–$100 million mixed-use project on a third of an acre adjacent to Priatek Plaza. All total, these projects will add more than two thousand new habitations to the downtown. This is a huge addition of new housing units, nearly twice the number in the Snell Isle neighborhood north of downtown, although on average it is expected there will be fewer people per unit.

It is important to emphasize that from a historical perspective, this is downtown *revitalization*. Historically, downtown was perhaps even more vibrant in terms of activity in the past, and the structure of past vitality continues to serve as the foundation for today's resurgence. Location, of course, is everything. Our founding city leaders recognized this by taking the downtown waterfront off the tax rolls and making a strategic decision to dedicate it as parkland. At one time, the Pier upland was far more developed than today, including the indoor Spa swimming pool, the Solarium for nude sun bathing and several other recreational amenities. Before the Vinoy, there was the three-hundred-room Soreno Hotel on Beach Drive. Both were located to take advantage of the Waterfront Parks, bay views and water-related recreation.

The genesis of urban development can be a complex process, at times difficult to interpret. No doubt the baseball stadium and other pre-1992 projects had their influence, both on the decision to invest in the Vinoy and in subsequent projects. But the Vinoy clearly played a special role in downtown revitalization, especially near the waterfront. Its narrative and ultimate success were definitely on the minds of the developers of the Cloisters, the Florencia and others wanting to make an investment in our city. The Vinoy is a testament to the important role historic preservation plays in both maintaining a city's sense of place and in generating economic development. Much has been written about the importance of preserving the environment and natural beauty of our nation, including that still remaining in our cities. Historic preservation should be similarly regarded. While our historic buildings are man-made, they, too, express beauty and enhance our quality of life.

The role of the Florida International Museum, opening three years after the Vinoy, was also prominent in downtown development, sparking restaurants, retail and even BayWalk. While the International Museum no longer exists, it was followed by an array of other prominent cultural institutions, including the new Dalí, an expanded Museum of Fine Arts, a renovated Mahaffey, the Chihuly Glass Collection and an increasingly energetic History Museum, to name a few. Tom James, CEO of Raymond James Financial, has committed $75 million for a new museum to exhibit his collection of western and wildlife art. Ruby Ciccarello of the Two Red Roses Foundation is building the largest arts and crafts museum in the nation next to the Synovus Bank on 3rd Avenue North. A new Pier is pending, and master planning is underway to further invigorate the storied downtown Waterfront Parks. These cultural resources not only attract visitors but also provide rich cultural opportunities for city residents, particularly those living in the downtown area. While the Vinoy was prominent in beginning the process of downtown revitalization, each subsequent development further added to the snowball effect, creating a synergy that both sustains development accomplishments previously achieved and boosts them further yet.

Sources: City of St. Petersburg, City Charter (1982, 1984), and "Major Downtown Development Projects List" (2014); Prudy Taylor Board, *The Renaissance Vinoy: St. Petersburg's Crown Jewel* (1999); *Evening Independent*, various dates but especially April 23, 1986; Walter P. Fuller, *St. Petersburg and Its People* (1972); *Tampa Bay Times*, various dates but especially November 7, 1984, August 10, 2002, August 1, 2012, November 21, 2014; Hotel News Resource, "US Hotel Occupancy Rate to Recover to Pre-Recession Levels in 2014 According to PKF," March 18, 2014; Gary Lantrip, "Profile: Frederick E. Guest II," *Tampa Bay Life* (September 1990); June Hurley Young, *The Vinoy: Faded Glory Renewed* (1999); and communications with Peter Belmont, Martin Normile, Craig McLaughlin and David Fischer. Also, many thanks to Elaine Normile, Renaissance Vinoy Hotel historian, for her extensive help and support.

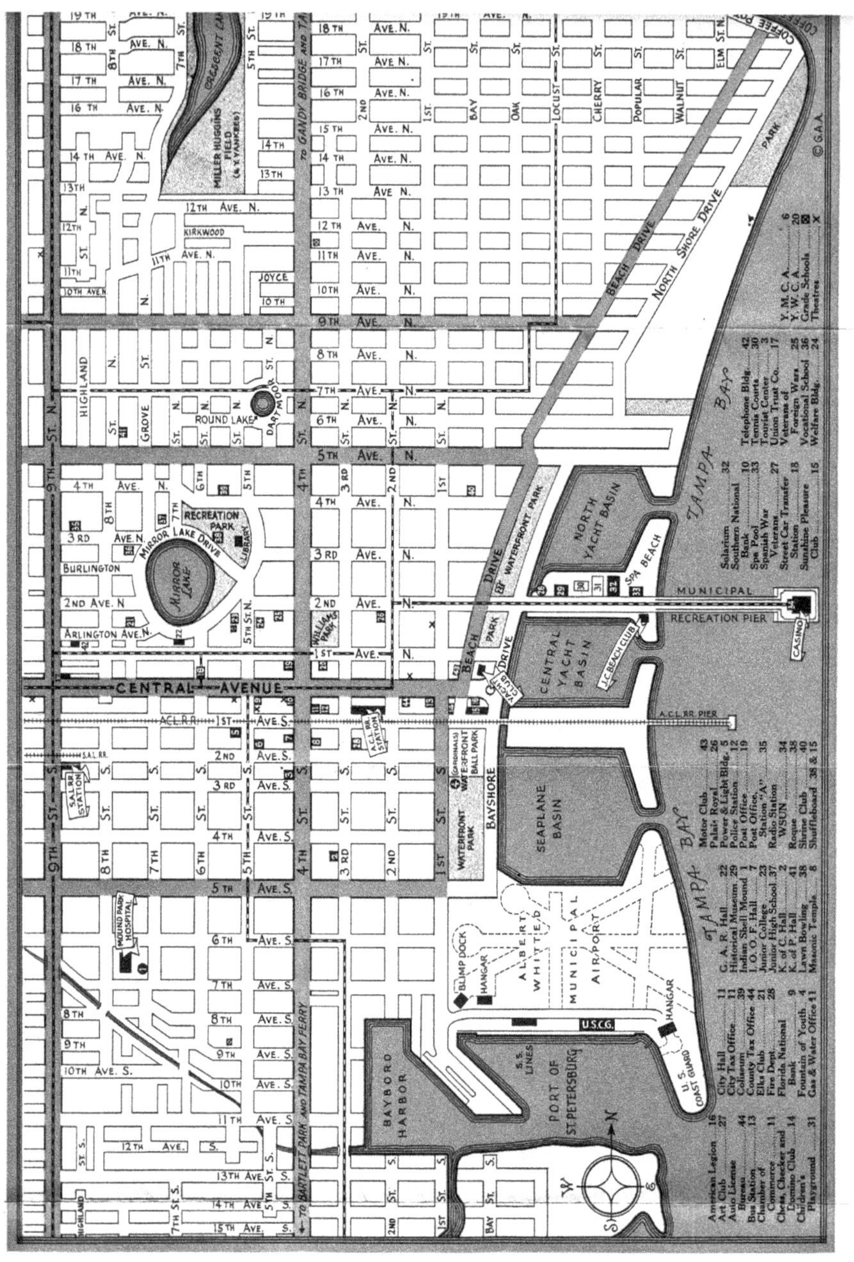

Map of Downtown St. Petersburg, 1937. Note that the Waterfront Park extends from 5th Avenue South to 5th Avenue North, with additional parkland at 7th and 13th Avenues North. *St. Petersburg Chamber of Commerce; courtesy Michaels Family Collection.*

Chapter 13

William Straub's Waterfront Revisited

It is well known that the father of our downtown Waterfront Parks is William L. Straub, the crusading editor of the *St. Petersburg Times*. It was Straub who successfully led a hard-fought struggle to preserve the downtown waterfront as a place of beauty for public use—part of the "City Beautiful Plan," as he called it. The original park was effectively acquired in December 1909 and formally dedicated a year later in December 1910.

Sometimes one gets the impression that Straub and his team only intended the downtown waterfront for green parkland and nothing else. This is far from the case. While Straub certainly held natural beauty and greenspace in high regard, he also supported a range of public buildings and amenities on the waterfront over his storied career in our city, dating from 1901 to 1939.

The Yacht Club

Part and parcel with the establishment of the downtown park was the dredging of the bay for use of pleasure boats and yachts. Even before completion of the acquisition of the waterfront lots for park usage, Straub and other community leaders met to form a Yacht Club (October 1909). Straub was selected secretary. The first outing was held with twenty boats participating in December 1909. Thereafter, the Yacht Club languished until completion of the Central Yacht Basin in 1916. At that time, the Yacht

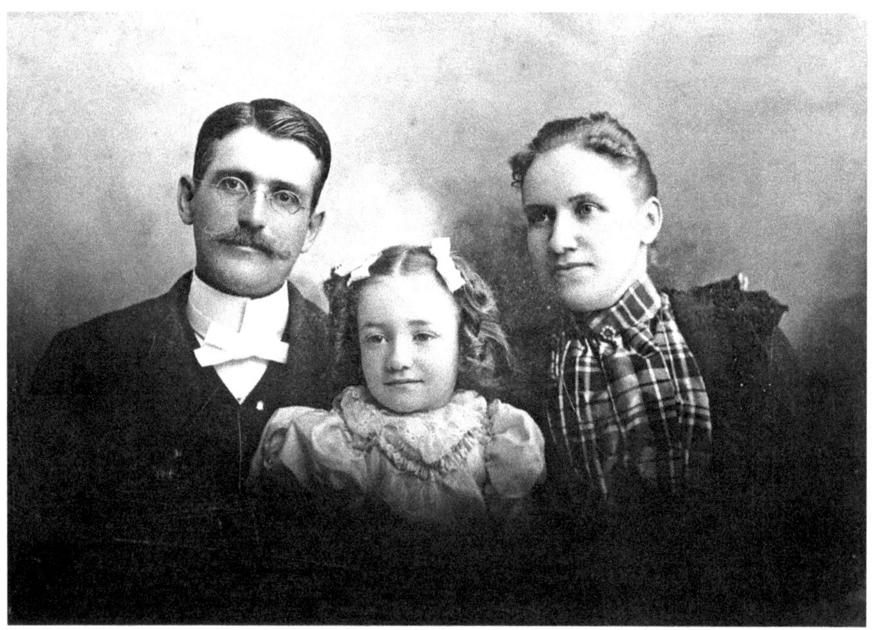

William L. Straub with his wife, Sarah, and his daughter, Blanche. Straub is widely recognized as the "Father of the Waterfront Parks," image 1899. *Courtesy St. Petersburg Museum of History.*

Club was revitalized, and Straub was again a participant. It was also at that time that the city and the Yacht Club entered into an agreement to lease part of Waterfront Park at Central and Bayshore for a clubhouse for thirty years at one dollar per year. The clubhouse was opened the following year. An addition was added to the north in 1922.

Straub lauded the Yacht Club building in his editorials. He noted there was "unanimous support" for the project and that the building of the clubhouse would "practically complete all the big essentials of the City Beautiful waterfront plans." He stated that the building of the Yacht Club would be "an immensely valuable enterprise for the whole city....Let there be no hitch or hesitation in building the Yacht Club House."

In 1963, the Yacht Club bought the city's interest in the property for $260,000. However, the deed contained a reverter clause stating that were the property to be no longer used by the club, the title would revert to the city. In 1986, the city vacated 1st Avenue North, which added an additional fifty feet to club property. In 1990, the Yacht Club sought to expand the footprint of the clubhouse. This was opposed by the *Times* and citizens wishing to maximize parkland and water views. In 1991,

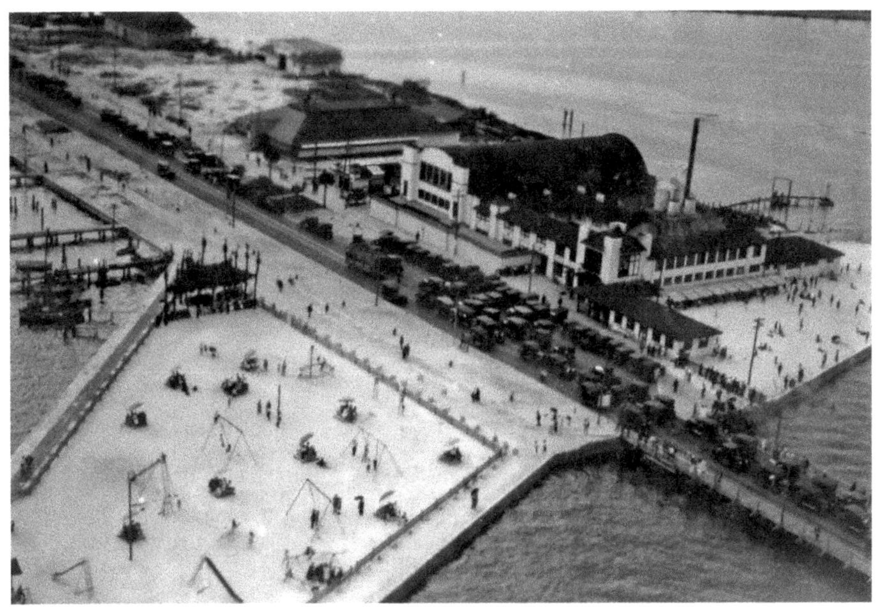

Early aerial view of approach to St. Petersburg Pier, showing children's playground, Spa Beach, the indoor Spa pool, the band pavilion and dance hall and Johnny Green's airboat hangar. Image circa 1923. *Courtesy St. Petersburg Museum of History.*

a compromise was agreed on allowing for the permitting of the larger clubhouse in exchange for the Yacht Club deeding its half of the vacated street back to the city.

In the 1970s, the Yacht Club also negotiated with the city an agreement to operate a sailing center for youth and adult sailing programs on Demens Landing. As part of this agreement, the city spent about $375,000 to construct a sailing facility there. The Yacht Club has since operated the facility, providing boats, equipment and a full-time staff under a series of facility management agreements. The club subsidized the center and its sailing programs to the extent of about $375,000 per year, not including hundreds of volunteer hours. Ownership of the sailing center remains with the city.

While the creation of a Yacht Club was part of Straub's vision for the waterfront from the beginning, it is noteworthy how protective of the park city government was nearly fifty years later. The city only leased the property, and while the property was later sold, the sale included a reverter clause that remains in force to this day. While city government itself did not object to a larger footprint in the 1990s, interests in the larger community did, resulting in a compromise that returned additional green space to the city.

THE PIERS, SPA, FIRST AIRLINE HANGAR, AQUARIUM, HISTORY MUSEUM, ART CLUB AND DANCE HALL

The waterfront was the site of several piers prior to the establishment of the parks. These included the original Railroad Pier built by Peter Demens and John C. Williams Sr. in 1888. Interestingly, this pier was not just for transportation but also featured a bathing pavilion for residents and hoped-for tourists. There was also the Brantley Pier, built in 1896 as an alternative to the Railroad Pier, which had been acquired by Henry Plant and his railroad monopoly. The Brantley also boasted a bathing pavilion. The Brantley was succeeded by the larger Electric Pier in 1905.

Just three years after the Waterfront Park was established, a city-owned and operated Municipal Pier was built, and this soon replaced the privately owned Electric Pier. This was the first of four city-owned piers, the others being the Million Dollar Pier, the Inverted Pyramid Pier and the pending Pier Park. It was also at this time that the basin was dredged and the area of land between Bayshore Drive and the present entrance to the pier filled. This area of filled land has been variously known as the north breakwater, the north mole, the pier approach and the upland. A "bathing pavilion," soon to become known as the Spa, was privately constructed on the fill leading out to the Pier. The Spa initially offered salt- and sulfur-water baths, a steam room with "hand and electric massage," a coffee room, a soda fountain and space for dances. Soon after the Spa opened, the city moved to regulate decorum at the facility and adjacent pier by forbidding one-piece bathing suits, "unless they were protected with a skirt which gives the same modest effect as a two-piece suit." Straub boosted this "splendid" pavilion, saying it would "delight" the public and "pay substantial revenue to the city." The initial lease called for the owner to pay the city between $500 and $1,000 per year, a substantial sum given that the Spa cost $10,000 to build. But the lease was soon renegotiated on terms very favorable to the owner, and the city eventually ended up paying the owner $160,000 to get the property back and operate it directly.

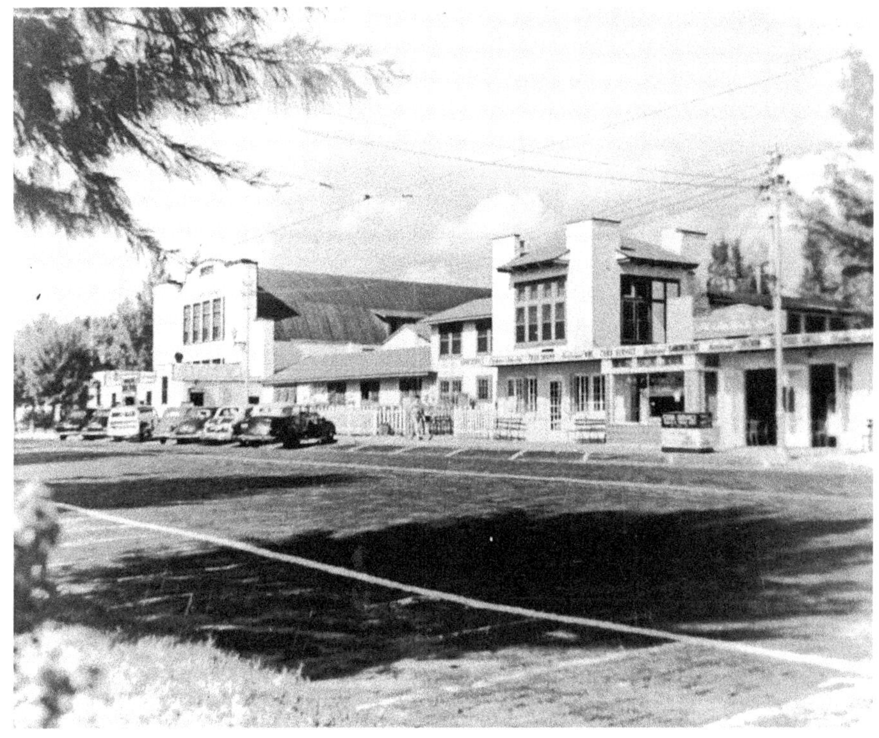

The Spa on the Pier Approach. Just three years after the establishment of the Waterfront Park, the Spa (large structure) and the Municipal Pier were built. Note the hamburger joint offering curb service to the right, image 1945. *Courtesy St. Petersburg Museum of History.*

The Spa was followed in 1914 by a hangar to service the airboats of the world's first airline, the St. Petersburg–Tampa Airboat Line. The hangar was built on the south side of the pier approach adjacent to the Central Yacht Basin by the city at a cost of approximately $400. Straub's *Times* enthusiastically reported on the airline's activities. An additional hangar was soon built near the airline hangar for Raymond V. Morris, who was training for international flying races with a new monoplane designed by Glenn Curtiss. One of these hangars was later used by early aviator Johnny Green for excursion flights and a flight school. By 1923, the hangar used by Green had been relocated to the north side of the pier approach. A second hangar was also constructed on the north side of the approach for Albert Whitted, after whom Albert Whitted Airport was named. About 1920, a privately operated aquarium was constructed on the approach. In 1922, this became the home of what is now called the St. Petersburg Museum of History, which occupies the site to this day. The museum building and the land on which it sits is owned by the city and leased to the museum. The museum is responsible for most of the operating costs and has, in fact, contributed substantially to capital improvements that benefit the city for which the museum has received no reimbursement.

The Art Club, precursor to today's Morean Arts Center, was located in a city-owned building at 201 Beach Drive Northeast beginning in 1923, and it operated there until the early 1960s, when the building was demolished. In 1961, the city donated four and a half acres of Straub Park, including the Art Club site, to the Museum of Fine Arts. The museum was designed by architect John Volk in the Florentine and Palladium styles.

The approach to the Pier also boasted a dance hall and banquet facility, originally known as the St. Petersburg Concert Band Pavilion and Dance Hall. The hall, which seated as many as five hundred people, was built in 1915 by the St. Petersburg Concert Band on land leased from the city. In 1919, lease payments amounted to $1,000 per month. At one point, the pavilion and dance hall came to be known as The Jitney. Later, the lease was acquired by early St. Petersburg pilot Johnny Green, and in 1922, the facility was renamed the Green Lantern. The facility was also used by the chamber of commerce for tourist society banquets. The pavilion and dance hall was demolished in 1929 and replaced by the Solarium. Other early pier approach amenities included a photo shop and children's playground.

WATERFRONT PARK STADIUM

The Boston Braves were enticed to the city in 1921 by the construction of Waterfront Field, a little north of today's Al Lang Stadium. This property was secured from the City Park Board on a ninety-nine-year lease. Local boosters paid for the 2,500-seat stadium. The president of the Braves told Mayor Al Lang that they would come if a new ballpark were built. St. Petersburg City officials urged residents to contribute to the cost of the ballpark, stating that the spring training publicity alone "is worth many times the cost of the ball field."

Straub was also an enthusiastic supporter of the waterfront stadium. He extended his congratulations to those involved. The proposal was first put forward by the local Rotary Club, which Straub himself had founded just a year before. He noted that the stadium plans called for the ballpark to be a "beauty spot instead of the high-boarded enclosure that so many ball parks become." He then went on to say that there are "plans for an environmental

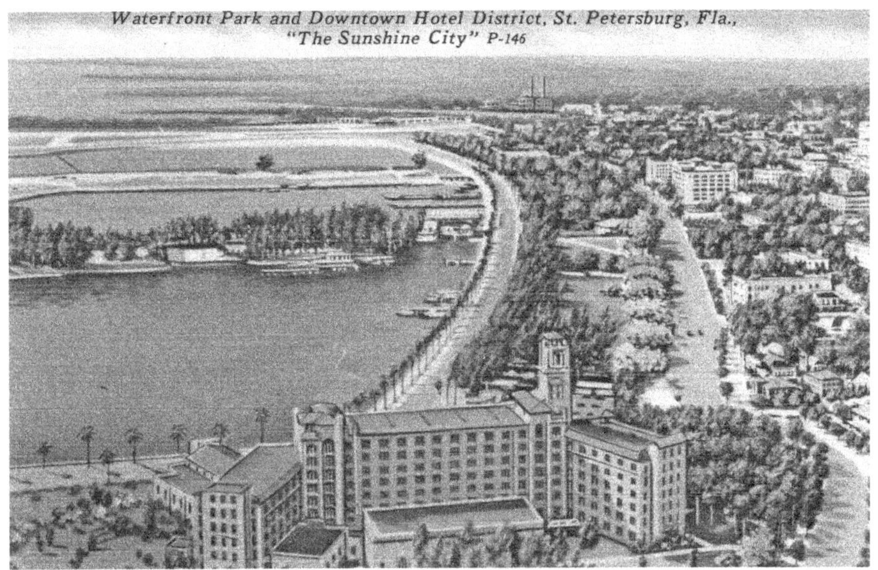

View of early downtown Waterfront Park as taken from the Vinoy Hotel looking south. Note the Soreno Hotel in the upper right, image circa 1940. *Tichnor Bros. Inc., Boston; courtesy Michaels Family Collection.*

fence and vines and hedge which will give the ball park the appearance of a real park and at the same time secure the purposes of an athletic field." Perhaps he was struggling a little with himself to fit the concept of the stadium into waterfront green space. Or perhaps his commitment to a beautiful publicly owned waterfront included buildings if they were attractive, as well as green space. In the same *Times* edition containing the previous quote, Straub also called for the establishment of a City Planning Board.

THE SOLARIUM

In 1930, the city again repackaged and pitched its most plentiful commodity: sunshine. A Solarium was built by the city at a cost of $15,000 to the west of the Spa on the site of the Green Lantern Recreation Building. Some thirty thousand people reportedly turned out for the dedication. Imagine, nude sun bathing in St. Petersburg in the 1930s! This was no doubt also seen at the time as a way to bring St. Petersburg out of the Great Depression. But building the Solarium was not without protest. Some argued that the Solarium was in direct competition with private enterprise and that if it were to be built there should be a public referendum.

Straub was also an enthusiastic supporter of both the Spa and the Solarium, and he advocated their direct operation by the city. "When city officials are quoted in favor of leasing waterfront property it is time to remind them that the general public interest comes first and that giving up the control by the municipality of such important properties as the Solarium and the Spa would undermine and possibly destroy some vital factors in the up-building of the tourist and other industries where public relations are of first importance.…Some of the most potent advertising in the north is built around the Solarium; sunbathing is considered one of the important healing agencies." This 1930 statement about not leasing public waterfront properties was a change from his earlier 1913 statement about the Spa in which he lauded the lease with a private operator.

CONCORDIUM

While Straub clearly deserves the lion's share of the credit for creation of the Waterfront Parks, C. Perry Snell also deserves significant recognition. Snell was the developer of what are now the Historic Old Northeast Neighborhood, Granada Terrace, Snell Isle and the Snell Arcade, to name just a few of his projects. In 1912, just two years after the dedication of the Waterfront Park, he made a tour of Europe giving special attention to how European resort cities developed their waterfronts. He noted that a major building providing for amusement and recreation was often located on the waterfront. He was particularly impressed with the Kurhaus Hotel in The Hague, Netherlands. Upon his return to St. Petersburg, as chair of the Waterfront Committee of the Board of Trade, he unveiled a new plan for the waterfront. This plan called for a museum, a clubhouse, a women's league building, a dance hall, a skating rink, a café, a bathing house and a new promenade pier. At the center of all this would be a two-thousand-seat auditorium and activities building to be called the Concordium. All of this would have been built on the site of the newly established Waterfront Park! The plan was heartily endorsed by William Straub, who called the plan "splendid," and unanimously approved by the city council. Architect George W. Stewart, who later designed the Open-Air Post Office at the corner of 4th Street and 1st Avenue North, was retained to implement the plan.

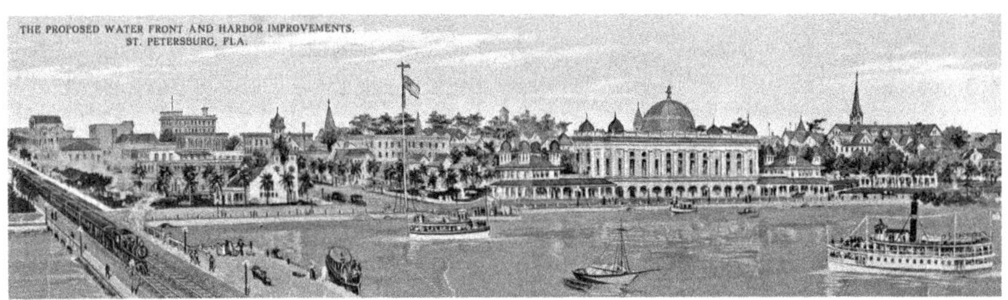

C. Perry Snell's 1912 Condordium Plan for the downtown Waterfront Park as illustrated by architect George W. Stewart. While the plan was never adopted, several features were later incorporated into the approach to the Pier, image 1913. *Courtesy Michaels Family Collection.*

Fortunately, for those who value the Waterfront Parks' greenspace, the Concordium Plan as envisioned was never implemented. But it did establish a direction for future development of the waterfront, although most of that development was along the approach to the pier: the History Museum, clubhouse, dance hall, café, bathing house and a new pier at the end. Straub later recognized a distinction between the Waterfront Park as it first stretched from 4th Avenue South to 5th Avenue North and the filled land creating the approach to the Pier. While he saw the city as having strong policies protecting the parkland between Beach Drive and Bayshore Drive, he observed that there was no policy or plan addressing the approach to the pier. In 1920, he noted that this "section of the city's waterfront has been set apart tacitly for the use of amusement enterprises" and advocated establishing a formal policy regarding its future development.

Straub's vision was not limited to St. Petersburg's waterfront but rather encompassed the entire city and soon the newly formed county of Pinellas. As early as 1913, a city advisory Park Board was established at the urging of Straub and others. Environmentalist and postmaster Roy Hanna chaired the new board. He and Straub contacted the Olmsted Brothers firm in Boston to develop a parks plan for the entire city. Olmsted Brothers was the nation's most prestigious landscape architecture firm at the time. It was the Olmsted brothers' father, Frederick Law Olmsted, who designed Central Park in New York City. The Park Board subsequently expanded its focus from the city to the county. Pinellas County had just been formed from part of Hillsborough County, and the opportunity seemed ripe for engaging the county as a whole in park conservation and planning rather than limiting efforts to St. Petersburg. In 1914, the Olmsted firm was subsequently hired by the new county commission. The firm sent its associate James Frederick

Dawson to undertake the plan, which took on his name. At the time, the powers of county government were limited, and in order to implement the Dawson Plan, it was necessary to establish an independent taxing board. The prospect of higher taxes and the establishment of an independent board caused the county commission to withdraw its support, and the plan was never implemented.

In 1920, Straub advocated for a City Planning Board in addition to the Park Board. This was established, and Straub became its first chair. The planning board, as did the park board before, turned for assistance to a preeminent expert, John Nolen. Nolen had been a student of Frederick Olmsted Jr., who taught landscape design at Harvard in addition to his landscape architecture practice. Nolen completed his city plan in 1923, Florida's first. It reflected much of the planning philosophy of the Olmsted brothers and their father. Completed in 1923, Nolen's plan envisioned St. Petersburg as a resort city, which necessitated preservation of the city's outstanding natural environmental features. He called for development of a park system that followed the creeks and Cross Bayou drainage canal, surrounded by a series of pleasure drives. Other features of his plan included a network of park blocks that would enable all residents to live within a half mile of natural green space, as well as axial boulevards leading downtown and development of Central Avenue as a grand boulevard. While the plan was defeated in a referendum in 1923, it nevertheless served as a catalyst for thoughtful discussion about St. Petersburg's future and as the basis for later city planning. Nolen's firm later proposed a zoning ordinance approved by the city in 1933.

Our city's downtown waterfront history and story is complicated. The creation of the downtown Waterfront Park was a purposeful, strategic decision by Straub, C. Perry Snell and other city leaders. It involved a thoughtful appraisal of our city's economic potential both as a tourist-oriented city and a city aspiring to provide quality of life for its residents. Public ownership of waterfront property was rare in the early 1900s. It took vision and courage to advocate for city ownership of the waterfront, an action that took valuable property off the immediate tax roles in exchange for long-term benefits. It involved early recognition that the waterfront was the city's primary asset and that if it were to be saved for parkland and public use, it was important to act before development occurred rather than after. Straub and others wandered at times from their vision, particularly with the Concordium Plan, but their original vision was nevertheless sustained. Straub's push to bring such preeminent landscape architects as Olmsted Brothers and John Nolen was a logical extension of his concern for preserving the natural beauty of the city. The balance of green space and public amenities such as museums and recreational facilities has been an ongoing struggle and continues to this day. Straub's vision involved both. Our early efforts at city planning were not immediately successful. The Dawson, Nolen and other plans reaching at least to the 1970s failed to be implemented. They were inspired in a way by Straub's accomplishment of preserving the scenic beauty of the waterfront and developing around it, a concept now referred to as New Urbanism. While these early plans failed, they positively influenced later planning efforts.

There is no doubt that Straub was a committed environmentalist who highly valued green space. In 1913, he editorialized regarding Florida's fields, forests and waters, "To the extent that we wisely or unwisely use the heritage of millions now in their infancy or yet to be born, will this generation be blessed or cursed by its heirs....We have no moral right to destroy any part of this great capital, instead it should be passed on with interest. It is not ours to squander." Straub also once said, "The struggle for preservation of the environment will only succeed if the community guards and protects the region's natural wonders." Most prominent among these wonders is our public waterfront lands.

Aside from our people, the city's greatest asset is the Downtown Waterfront Parks, including the Pier. Straub's vision of the downtown waterfront is complex. There is no doubt that he deeply appreciated the importance of green parkland, but this did not exclude the appropriateness of well-designed institutional structures on the waterfront, particularly on the approach to the Pier. On the other hand, he would probably be even more zealous about protecting our open green spaces and natural beauty today than he was in his time, yet he would be pleased that the original Waterfront Park has been substantially expanded over time. Straub's call for clear policies and protections regarding the Waterfront Parks System remains germane to this day. Current policies are a mixture of referendum requirements, limited lease options, land use plans, zoning regulations and a recently adopted Downtown Waterfront Master Plan. Current zoning for parts of the Pier Approach and some other sections of the Waterfront Parks System even allows for condos, offices and hotels. These policies and documents are difficult for the public to understand and remain in need of greater clarity and coherence. This could possibly be achieved by developing a special comprehensive plan land use designation and zoning for the downtown Waterfront Parks System.

The recently adopted master plan includes what are referred to as five "overarching themes" or "dimensions." The dimensions address developing a sustainable relationship between the natural and built environments;

WILLIAM L. STRAUB

Straub left his stamp on our city in more ways than just the Waterfront Parks. He campaigned for better roads and sidewalks, for better public schools, for a more humane penal system, for a city-manager style government and for the creation of the first public Park Board. He was instrumental in bringing about the creation of Pinellas County, breaking it off from Hillsborough County (1911). And it was not just what he did for our city but also the way in which he did it. He pushed for positive change but brought it about in a way that allowed for reasonable compromise and mutual respect. In 1902, he probably saved the lives of the officers of a failed bank when they were the target of angry depositors. He helped to mediate a dispute over the incorporation of our city in 1903. He obtained the support of Clearwater for creation of Pinellas County by not insisting the county seat be located in St. Petersburg, even though our city was much larger. In the words of his great-grandson Frank Straub Starkey, "He was and continues to be a model of civic responsibility for us all." As historian Walter P. Fuller put it, "Straub was the greatest influence for the development of the community ever to appear on the scene."

expanding St. Petersburg as a waterfront destination; diversifying the activities of the waterfront to meet a growing community's needs; leveraging the economic potential of in-water and upland areas along the water's edge; and creating continuous linkages, service oriented parking and transit and increased access to the waterfront. Also included in the plan are "development opportunity sites" together with specific opportunity site recommendations. The plan provides a planning framework for making decisions regarding the future development of the Waterfront Parks System. While some opportunity recommendations are controversial, many of the suggestions offered are promising. Mayor Rick Kriseman, in his introductory statement to the plan, spoke of the importance of achieving a "sustainable relationship between nature and possible downtown development" and noted that the plan calls for "enhancing the experience of the water, our park system, and ensures our downtown remains economically vibrant." These are familiar themes that continue to be challenging to balance.

WATERFRONT STRUCTURES

1913–26	Municipal Recreation Pier
1913–62	The Spa
1914–26	The Benoist and Johnny Green Hangars
1915–29	Concert Band Pavilion & Dance Hall
1917–to date	Yacht Club
1920–to date	History Museum (originally an Aquarium)
1921–47	Waterfront Park Stadium
1923–63	Art Club
1925/26–67	The Million Dollar Pier
1930–61	Solarium
1947–77	First Al Lang Stadium
1961/1965–to date	Fine Arts Museum
1963/65–2004	Bayfront Center (Times Arena)
1963/65–to date	Mahaffey Theater
1971–2015	Inverted Pyramid Pier
1977–to date	Second Al Lang Field
1982–to date	Dalí Museum
(dates unknown)	Doc Webb Sr. Citizens Center

Note: Slash dates indicate first site acquisition or construction start dates followed by opening dates.

Sources: Raymond Arsenault, *St. Petersburg and the Florida Dream: 1888–1950* (1988/1996); Rick Baker, *Mangroves to Major League: A Timeline of St. Petersburg, Florida* (2000); William C. Ballard, ed., *A Nautical Heritage—The St. Petersburg Yacht Club Story: 1909–2009* (1989); Walter P. Fuller, *St. Petersburg and Its People* (1972); Karl H. Grismer, *The Story of St. Petersburg* (1948); Will Michaels, "William Straub's Waterfront Revisited," *Northeast Journal* (2010); Thomas Reilly, *Jannus: An American Flyer* (1997); the *St. Petersburg Times*, various dates but especially November 7, 1912, March 15, 1913, October 4, 1913, October 9, 1913, December 12, 1913, September 17, 1914, July 9, 1916, May 16, 1920, July 16, 1921, November 4, 1929, October 12, 1929, February 3, 1930, September 23, 1931, September 30, 1962; R. Bruce Stephenson, *Visions of Eden* (1997); W.L. Straub, *History of Pinellas County Florida* (1929); and communication with William C. Ballard.

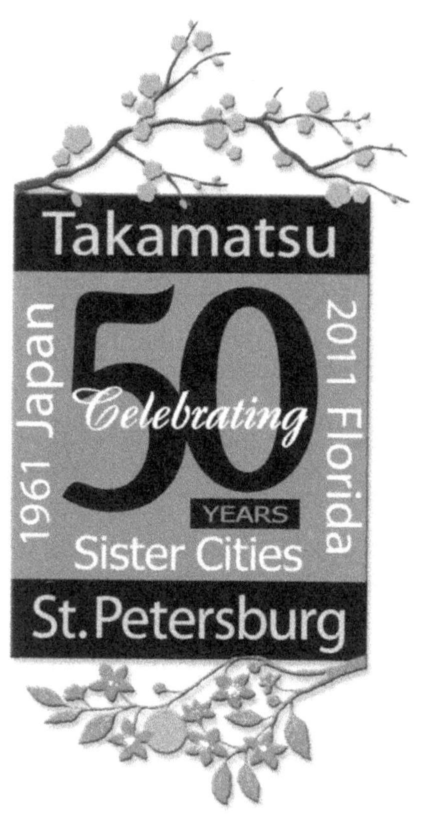

Logo designed to celebrate the fiftieth anniversary of the St. Petersburg–Takamatsu Sister Cities Partnership, image 2011. *Courtesy City of St. Petersburg.*

Chapter 14

Our Sister City

Takamatsu

In the beginning, some in St. Petersburg were not all that enthused about becoming a Sister City with Takamatsu, Japan. It was 1961, only sixteen years since the end of World War II. Many still had bitter memories of Japan from the war. On the other hand, Takamatsu had bitter memories, too, especially dating from July 4, 1945, when about 80 percent of the city was destroyed in a U.S. bombing attack.

The Sister Cities Program was founded by President Dwight D. Eisenhower in 1956 at the White House Summit on Citizen Diplomacy. Eisenhower envisioned a network of sister cities that would be a "champion for peace and prosperity by fostering bonds between people from different communities around the world." He believed that "people from different cultures could understand, appreciate, and celebrate their differences while building partnerships that would lessen the chance of new conflicts." St. Petersburg's Sister City relationship with Takamatsu, Japan, was one of the first Sister City Programs in the United States.

According to the City Sister City Handbook, the history of the sister city relationship between Takamatsu and St. Petersburg began on January 30, 1959. On that day, Takamatsu city assemblyman Kazuo Matsuda first brought up the idea of a city affiliation with a foreign country. But it was not until 1961 that a request was formally made to the Ministry of Foreign Affairs of Japan for recommendations of potential sister cities in the United States. The ministry solicited the help of U.S. ambassador to Japan Douglas MacArthur II (nephew of General Douglas MacArthur) and the Japanese ambassador in Washington, Koichiro Asakai, in selecting an appropriate city. St. Petersburg was recommended.

The two cities were matched because of their similarity. Both were incorporated as municipalities less than one hundred years before, although Takamatsu traces its history as a city back to the twelfth century. Both faced the water, had a similar climate and were tourist cities. The populations and city square miles were about the same size at that time. Also coincidentally, Takamatsu means "tall pine" in Japanese, and the numerous pine trees in Pinellas County contributed to the name "Pinellas"; in St. Petersburg itself, the southernmost part of the city is called "Pinellas Point." The name derives from the Spanish *Punta de Pinal*, or "Point of Pines."

Takamatsu is located on the island of Shikoku and is the capital city of the prefectural government, somewhat similar to our counties. It is a port city located on the Seto Inland Sea. Takamatsu now has a population of about 420,000 persons, and the prefecture has a population of about 980,000 people. The city enjoys a high concentration of branch offices of major Japanese companies, and it contains most of the national government's regional offices for Shikoku. It is also noted for its "bonsai masters," growers of traditional bonsai pine trees.

On June 1, 1961, Takamatsu mayor Teruta Kunito made a formal proposal to St. Petersburg to become a Sister City. The St. Petersburg City Council approved the proposal on September 14 on the recommendation of newly elected mayor Herman W. Goldner. The Takamatsu City Assembly gave final approval the following month. Mayor Goldner then asked his in-laws, Emilie and Earl Munyan, to visit Takamatsu as goodwill ambassadors. Upon arrival, they were met by enthusiastic crowds of Takamatsu citizens and city officials waving the U.S. and Japanese flags at the city port. They stayed at Mayor Kunito's residence and visited city hall, Ritsurin Park, Mount Yashima and the art studio of Joshin Ishoi, a designated "National Treasure" of Japan. At that time, Joshin was working on the Pine Tree Ceremonial Water Jug, a delicately lacquered work of art. It was later sent to Mayor Goldner as a gift. In October 1961, St. Petersburg received its first visitors from Takamatsu, a delegation of engineers visiting the United States to study power transmission.

Sister City affairs in Takamatsu have been handled from the beginning by city government. In St. Petersburg, they were originally handled by a private organization called the Sister City Committee. This Blue Ribbon Committee was chaired by Lowell Brandle of the *St. Petersburg Times* and included the mayor, Superintendent of Schools Floyd Christian, chamber

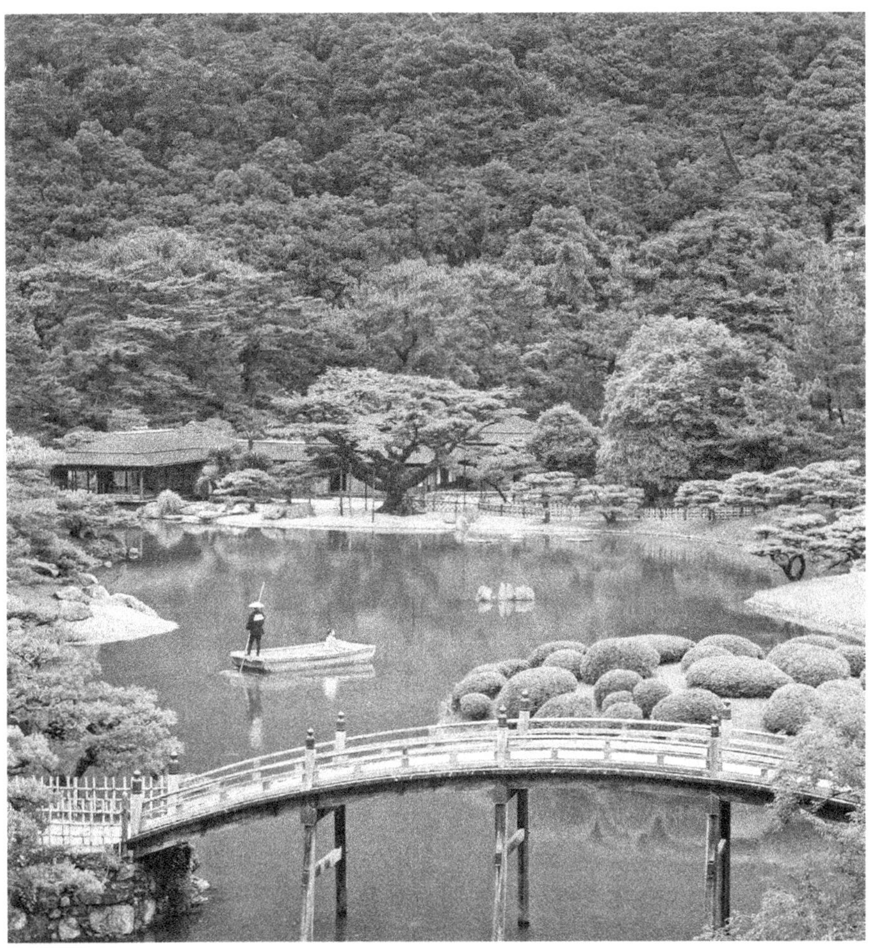

Ritsurin Garden in Takamatsu, Japan, St. Petersburg's Sister City. Ritsurin Garden dates from the 1620s and is one of the best traditional gardens in Japan. Other nearby attractions include the Chi Chu Art Museum, designed by Tadao-Ando and displaying works by Claude Monet, Walter De Maria and James Turell; and the Lee Ufan Museum, also designed by Tadao-Ando and displaying the works of Lee Ufan. *Courtesy City of Takamatsu.*

president Byron Shouppe, architect William B. Harvard, businessmen Oscar R. Kruetz and Jim Walter and others. Gay Blair White, who first documented the St. Petersburg–Tampa Airboat Line of 1914 as the world's first airline, served as marketing consultant. Since 1983, they have been handled by the city's International Relations Committee. The committee is composed of interested citizens and a member of the city council.

The year after signing the sister city agreement, the two cities officially established an exchange program, initially exchanging "friendship ambassadors." Takamatsu's first designated "Ambassador-of-Goodwill" to St. Petersburg was Professor Fukuhichi Uemura of Kagawa University. He arrived in August 1962. The welcoming program was planned by chamber of commerce president Byron Shouppe and architect William B. Harvard. It included a large delegation to meet the ambassador at Tampa International Airport, including Girl Scouts, Brownies, Cub Scouts and Explorers. Activities included a reception at city hall, a dinner hosted by Mayor Goldner and tours of Tampa Bay, Presbyterian College (now Eckerd College) and the YMCA. In the tradition of the Japanese cherry trees planted on the National Mall in Washington, Professor Uemura and Mayor Goldner planted an orchid tree at Mirror Lake near city hall. This planting of a "friendship tree" has continued throughout the history of the Sister City Program. A *Times* article reporting Uemura's tour noted that "color movies will be taken during all his visit." St. Petersburg's first "Ambassador-at-Large" was Clinton I. Bates, a retired banker and Rotarian. After his first visit, he spent two months of every year in Takamatsu at his own expense. He was presented with so many gifts of welcome that his spare bedroom in St. Pete became a virtual "Japanese Museum."

Takako Tayama Lutz, in her short paper on the history of the sister cities, wrote in 1993 that "Takamatsu took the relationship seriously from the beginning, and the citizens were willingly involved in it." She noted that a Takamatsu student, Toshiaki Katayama, wrote to St. Petersburg's mayor asking for a St. Petersburg history book so he could translate it, and the mayor sent the book *St. Petersburg: An Informal History* by county attorney Page S. Jackson (1962). Katayama was the first citizen of Takamatsu to write to St. Petersburg Sister City officials. The student also solicited letters from St. Pete residents wanting information about Takamatsu, and his name and address was printed in the *Times*. In 1965, this same student rode a bike from Los Angeles to St. Petersburg, by way of New York, arriving after eighty-one days on the road. The *Times* reported that "he arrived in the teeth of a gale, his shoes falling off his feet, with only $1." Regarding some parts of the western end of his trip, Katayama noted, "There are no places in Japan where you can be so alone." The trip was supported by the Takamatsu Sister City Committee, Takamatsu mayor Kunito, Sophia University in Tokyo and Minolta Camera.

A Student Exchange Program has been operated by the city since 1984. The city's International Relations Committee selects one to two high

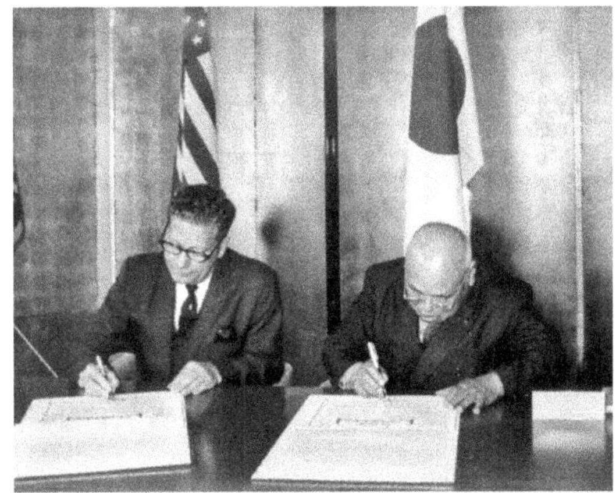

Mayor Herman Goldner and Mayor Teruta Kunito sign the Sister City Agreement in Takamatsu pledging active and lasting cultural and economic exchange between the two cities, image 1967. *Courtesy City of Takamatsu.*

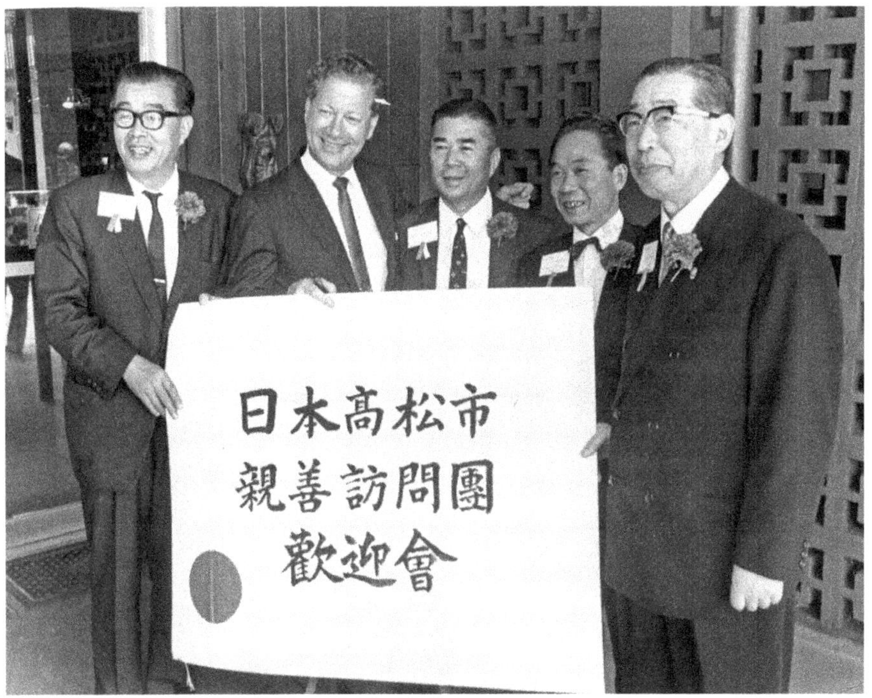

Mayor Herman Goldner receives an invitation to visit Takamatsu, Japan. *Left to right*: Mitami Kagawa, Mayor Goldner, Takeo Yamagurchi, Yoshitake Tsunetani and Dr. Tadahiko Tsuboi. Mayor Goldner was the first mayor to visit Takamatsu, image 1965. *Courtesy* Tampa Bay Times.

school juniors who are residents of St. Petersburg as goodwill ambassadors to Takamatsu. Selected students spend up to three weeks in Takamatsu. Typically, students visit Japan for about ten days in July. City staff makes travel arrangements, and all international travel costs are paid by the city. Students are hosted by families in Takamatsu. Students are expected to pay for their personal living expenses, such as transportation, visits to local attractions, meals in restaurants and so on. But ability to pay is not a requirement, and financial assistance is available.

While in Japan, students have an official meeting with the mayor of Takamatsu, attend high school with Japanese students, represent the city as goodwill ambassadors and share information about our city and culture with Japanese students and others. Students experience typical Japanese family life, culture, customs and local sights while living with host families. Since the relationship started in 1961, St. Petersburg has sent fifty-one student ambassadors to Takamatsu. Takamatsu has sponsored a similar program beginning in 2008 and has since sent twenty-three students to St. Petersburg. Its students usually come to St. Pete in July and are also hosted by local families.

From the beginning, educational and cultural activities were emphasized. At various times, schoolchildren in St. Pete and Takamatsu exchanged artworks, handcrafts and poem books. Schools, including Boca Ciega, Disston and Maximo, became "Sister Schools" with matched schools in Takamatsu. Gift exchanges became a tradition. On one occasion, St. Petersburg presented Takamatsu with a baseball signed by New York Yankees players Roger Maris and Mickey Mantle. At the time, the Yankees spring trained in St. Pete. For the fortieth anniversary, St. Pete sent a youth baseball team of fifteen boys called the St. Pete Rays of Fossil Park. They were matched against the Takamatsu Dragons. The "Friendship Games" ended in a tie. Also for the fortieth anniversary, the St. Petersburg Museum of History displayed a special exhibit on the Sister Cities Program, curated by Mary Anna Murphy, called "East Meets West: From St. Petersburg to Takamatsu Celebrating 40 Years of a Sister City Partnership."

In 1962, a generous donor in St. Petersburg funded a four-year scholarship to be used by Takamatsu teachers at Eckerd College (then Florida Presbyterian College). Hasui Nobuaki, a teacher from Takamatsu Daichi High School, was the first person sent to St. Pete to attend Eckerd College. Eckerd College, through a related program, has sent forty-eight graduates to live and teach English in Japan for an academic year. One of these was Mayor Goldner's son, Michael, who traveled to Takamatsu in

1969. He later observed that at that time the Japanese people were "in the midst of a cultural change so massive as to be almost unimaginable to the Westerner. After the War their entire outlook on life had to change." Also, city employees from Takamatsu spent several months at Eckerd College and then with the city, rotating through various departments learning about our municipal government. The interns also participated in cultural programs in local elementary and secondary schools.

Over the years, St. Petersburg has sent delegations to Takamatsu, including city council representatives and mayors, and Takamatsu has sent its delegations to St. Pete. The first St. Petersburg mayor to visit Takamatsu was Herman Goldner in 1967. Mayor Goldner visited again in 1972 as a part of a thirty-day world tour. Mayor Randy Wedding visited Takamatsu in 1974 as part of a family vacation. Mayor Nobuo Waki made his first visit to St. Petersburg in 1978. He returned again thirteen years later in 1991 to commemorate the thirtieth anniversary. Mayor Corrine Freeman visited Takamatsu in 1984. Among the gifts she presented to Mayor Waki were baseball suits from the St. Louis Cardinals and New York Mets. Both teams called St. Petersburg their spring training home at the time. Mayor Robert L. Ulrich visited the city in 1989 while attending a trade show on behalf of the U.S. Conference of Mayors. In 1990, Mayor Ulrich attended Takamatsu's centennial celebration and Sister City Fair. In 2008, Mayor Rick Baker traveled to Takamatsu.

Raising funds to support the Sister City Program has always been a challenge for St. Petersburg. Both the city and private donations have sustained the program over the years. For example, in 2008, in the midst of the Great Recession, the little funding included in the city budget for the city's International Program was completely eliminated. It was then that the Rays infielder baseball star Akinori (Aki) Iwamura stepped up to the plate and provided about $10,000 to fund the annual summer high school exchange for two years.

The fiftieth anniversary of the Sister City Program was held in 2011. For that occasion, Takamatsu sent a large delegation of more than eighty persons to St. Pete. The president of Takamatsu University, Masamichi Tsukuda, led the "Citizens Delegation," and Mayor Hideto Onishi led the "Official Delegation." A highlight of the celebration in St. Petersburg included the traditional tree planting ceremony. Also, there was a bonsai plant exchange between Perkins Elementary School and Kinashi elementary school in Takamatsu. A grand banquet was held at the Museum of Fine Arts. Mayor Bill Foster and former mayor Rick Baker both attended. The

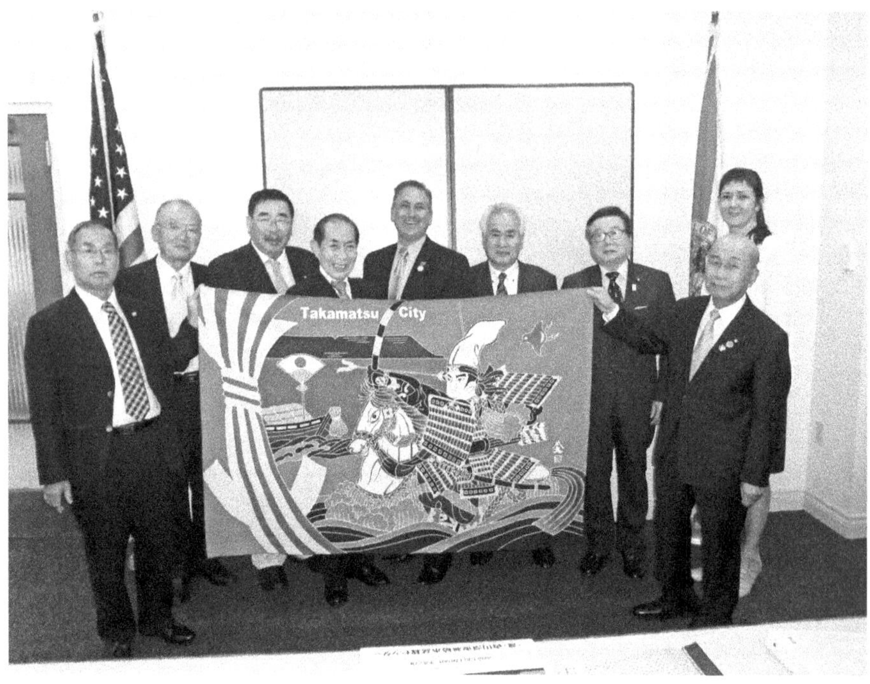

Takamatsu City Assembly delegation presents St. Petersburg mayor Rick Kriseman with Takamatsu traditional Iwaibata craft flag in 2014. *Left to right*: Yukio Yoshimine, Masao Tsuji, Yoji Kagawa, Mitsumasa Ohashi, Mayor Kriseman, Kozo Futagawa, Masanobu Kawasaki, Elizabeth Brinklow and Hitoshi Hata. *Courtesy City of St. Petersburg.*

author's daughter, Jeanne Michaels, fluent in Japanese, served as interpreter for Mayor Baker. Mayor Bill Foster also attended the celebrations in Takamatsu. He remembered the city rolling out the red carpet for the St. Petersburg delegation. "There was no want or need that was unmet." The city was decorated with banners commemorating the occasion. Art drawn by students at Anabuki College depicting St. Petersburg was displayed throughout Takamatsu's largest shopping mall. Foster reflected, "The people of Takamatsu truly understand the significance of art, education, literature, and culture, and because of this a Sister City relationship is very meaningful to them. The cultural exchanges of young people in particular, either as students or teachers, have been the most important aspect of the Sister Cities Program. And it's our humble contribution towards world peace."

Former mayor Foster also remembered a large metal bas-relief mural in Takamatsu commemorating the Sister Cities Program. The mural shows typical images from St. Petersburg, including the old Skyway Bridge, the

Pier, a pelican and palm trees. A similar commemorative monument or work of public art deserves to be raised in St. Petersburg to commemorate this enduring Sister Cities relationship.

Sources: *St. Petersburg Times*, various dates; Veda Heller, "Takamatsu, Japan/St. Petersburg, Florida Sister Cities 1961–1986," unpublished paper, 1986?; Takako Tayama Lutz, "Sister Cities: St. Petersburg, Florida—Takamatsu, Japan: An Analysis," unpublished paper, 1993; Mary Anna Murphy, "East Meets West: From St. Petersburg to Takamatsu Celebrating 40 years of a Sister City Partnership," unpublished text for exhibit at the St. Petersburg Museum of History, 2001; and communications with Bill Foster, Virginia Rowell, Wayne Atherholt, Jeanne Michaels and Mariko Kimura of the City of Takamatsu. (Note: The spelling of Japanese names in English has changed over the years. The author has endeavored to use contemporary spellings.)

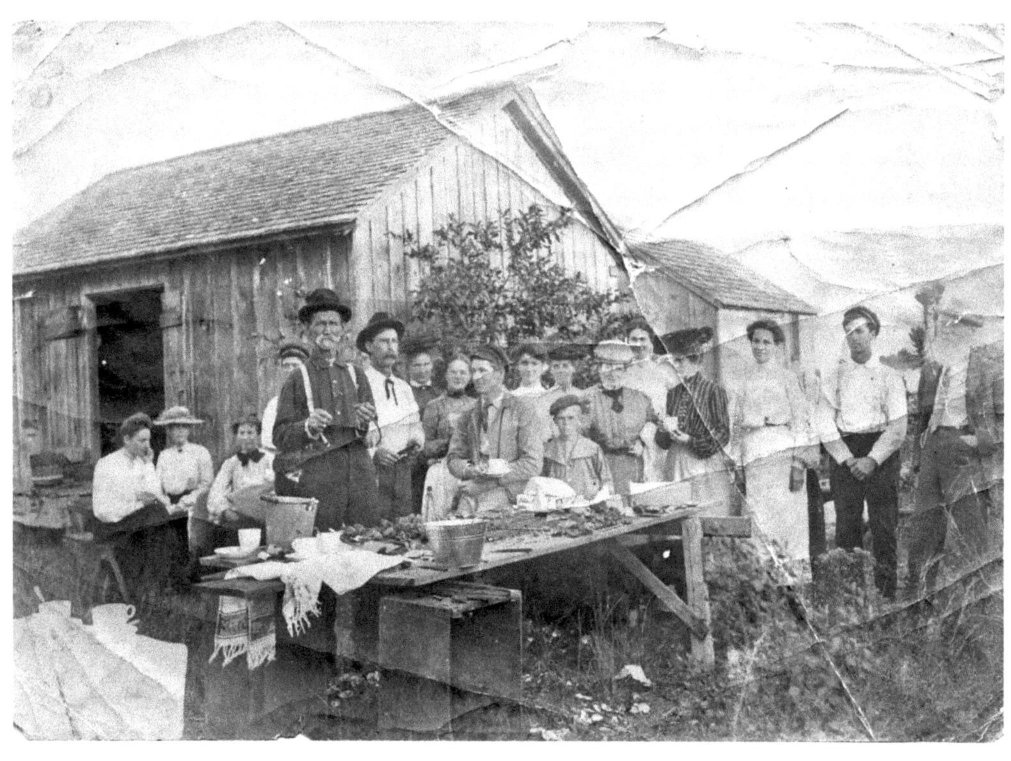

Oyster roast at Big Bayou. The Bethell clan and friends gather to honor patriarch John A. Bethell (standing with suspenders), image 1890. *Courtesy St. Petersburg Museum of History.*

Chapter 15

Much to Be Thankful For

Thanksgiving has a long history. Some trace the earliest documented Thanksgiving celebration back to 1565 in St. Augustine, Florida. Others venerate the pilgrims at Plymouth in 1621. George Washington declared a day of Thanksgiving in 1787. As a holiday, Thanksgiving was celebrated somewhat haphazardly until Abraham Lincoln standardized it in 1863 as the last Thursday in November. This worked fairly well until 1939, when Franklin Roosevelt decided to move it up to the fourth Thursday in November to allow more shopping days before Christmas, an idea to help us get out of the Great Depression. Congress itself reaffirmed the fourth Thursday in 1941.

But how was Thanksgiving celebrated in pioneer St. Petersburg? One of the earliest newspaper accounts is for 1902. For that Thanksgiving, the various churches of the city joined together to hold a "union" Thanksgiving. The *St. Petersburg Times* described it as "most appropriate, beautiful and impressive throughout. The great stage was magnificently decorated with products peculiar to the clime, palms, moss and great banks of fruit and flowers…the day may perhaps be set down as the most appropriately observed of any Thanksgiving in some years." But what about before the twentieth century—the late 1800s? How was Thanksgiving celebrated then, before there were churches in St. Pete? Not a lot has been written about the holiday during this period. For the most part, we can only speculate. But one thing is for certain: there was a lot of food to be cooked and eaten, and not just on Thanksgiving.

Rita Slaght Gould, in her work *Pioneer St. Petersburg: Life in and Around 1888*, described cooking in very early St. Petersburg. Many early pioneers cooked on hearths or "scaffold stoves." These consisted of a frame of pine logs approximately three feet wide and four feet square. Sand was poured inside and on top of this frame. The outside was covered with clay or marl so it would not ignite. The cooking fire was lit on top of the sand. These stoves were often located outside the house for reasons of safety. Some pioneers had iron grills on which to place their pots and other utensils. Those without them placed their skillets or Dutch ovens with short legs beside the fire and surrounded them with embers to ensure heat. Cast-iron cookware was commonly used. It maintained a steady heat, allowing food to simmer for hours. Large pots and kettles hung over the fire. Three-legged "spiders," the equivalent of today's frying pans, sat amid the coals. "Bake kettles," Dutch ovens with flat, rimmed lids, allowed coals to be placed on top as well as below.

All this preceded the introduction of cast-iron wood-burning stoves. "Adjusting the amount of heat put out by the burners was…difficult, and one could be burned if he or she were not careful. Soot was ever present." After the railroad was established in St. Pete in 1888, tourists began to come. Some of these were referred to as "coal-oil tourists" because most of them cooked on little stoves that burned kerosene, or coal-oil, as it was called in the South. All in all, as Rita Gould described it, "cooking was a chore" that began in the early morning from scratch.

Early St. Petersburg settlers did not often go without food. The climate offered a year-round growing season. Fish and game were plentiful. And there were a few small stores for what could not be grown, hunted or fished, but they did not have much to offer. Early settler John A. Bethell described the Pinellas Point area after the Civil War: "There were deer, bear, 'coons, possums, rabbits, squirrels, turkeys, geese, ducks, whooping cranes, blue and white cranes, curlew, quail, plover, snipe, etc. Besides these there were panthers and wildcats by the hundreds, and 'gators just as plentiful. All one had to do was to load his gun and go off from his enclosure, so as not to shoot any of his family, and kill a turkey or some other kind of game for dinner…I have stood on my porch and shot turkeys while eating my tomatoes." The Goose Pond, now the area known as Central Plaza, "was a noted place for geese in their season…I have seen these flats literally covered with geese, possibly a thousand or more." Bethell added to his account, "We never in those days killed game for profit or for the fun of it…but just what was absolutely necessary for home consumption" or, as he went on to say, to protect the domestic stock of hogs.

Another early pioneer extolled the virtues of gophers. The reference is believed to be to gopher turtles. "Most of you have never eaten it, but soup made from gophers—they burrow holes in the land—but is one of the finest of meats for soups. They are cleaner than a pig or chicken. They get up early in the morning, crawl out and eat only the tenderest shoots of grass that come up during the night."

Most early settlers had gardens to supplement their diets. These produced sweet potatoes, turnip greens, black-eyed peas, papaws, corn, hominy (grits), beans, eggplant, kohlrabi (cabbage), strawberries, pumpkins and sea grapes when they turned purple. Also, there were avocados (known as alligator pears or green pears), pomegranates, oranges, grapefruit, lemons, limes, figs, guava, bananas, coconuts, dates, citrons and loquat.

Of course, the waters of the bays and gulf were just as filled with fish as the forests were filled with game. In 1886, guests at the Waldorf Hotel in Disston City (now Gulfport) complained that they could not sleep at night because of all the noise made by the fish on the flats. David Griner, an early settler, had to abandon his cabin on the bank of Coffee Pot Bayou because the fish kept him awake at night. Historian Karl Grismer related that many old-timers told of seeing schools of fish so large they almost filled the bays. Pioneer George Lizotte "told of having seen one school which entered Boca Ciega [Bay] through the pass in the morning, kept moving northward all day, and was still in sight when darkness fell." The bays also contained some of the finest oyster beds in the nation, as well as delicious clams and scallops—"Enough shell fish for a dozen meals could be gathered in less than half an hour."

Some of this bounty was eventually sold to Cuban and Key West traders. Grismer recorded the prices paid in 1874: mullet, one cent; gophers, five cents; turtles weighing one hundred pounds or more, fifty cents; sweet potatoes, fifteen cents per bushel; pumpkins, one cent; green peas, thirty-five cents per bushel; shelled corn, twenty cents per bushel; lobster, five cents each; and stone crabs, ten cents a dozen.

When was the first Thanksgiving celebrated in St. Petersburg? We will probably never know. But we do know that many early pioneers who lived here did enjoy, and were no doubt thankful for, the natural bounty the land and waters had to offer. We are no less thankful today.

Sources: John A. Bethell, *Bethell's History of St. Petersburg* (1914/1962); Rita Slaght Gould, *Pioneer St. Petersburg: Life in and Around 1888* (1987); Karl H. Grismer, *The Story of St. Petersburg* (1948); Sandra W. Rooks, *Black America Series, St. Petersburg Florida* (2003); and the *St. Petersburg Times*, various dates.

Selected Bibliography

For unpublished works, periodicals and other sources, see the notes at the end of each chapter.

Apple, Marty. *Pinstripe Empire: The New York Yankees from Before the Babe to After the Boss*. New York: Bloomsbury, 2012.

Arsenault, Raymond. *St. Petersburg and the Florida Dream: 1888–1950*. Gainesville: University Press of Florida, 1996. Originally published in 1988.

Ayers, R. Wayne. *St. Petersburg the Sunshine City*. Charleston, SC: Arcadia Publishing, 2001.

———. *Tampa Bay's Gulf Beaches*. Charleston, SC: Arcadia Publishing, 2002.

Baker, Rick. *Mangroves to Major League: A Timeline of St. Petersburg, Florida*. St. Petersburg, FL: Southern Heritage Press, 2000.

———. *The Seamless City*. Washington, D.C.: Regency Publishing, 2011.

Beim, George, and Julia Ruth Stevens. *Babe Ruth: A Daughter's Portrait*. Dallas, TX: Taylor Publishing Company, 1998.

Bethell, John A. *Bethell's History of Pinellas Point*. St. Petersburg, FL: Great Outdoors Publishing, 1962. Originally published in 1914.

Betz, Myrtle Scharrer. *Yesterday I Lived in Paradise: The Story of Caladesi Island*. Tampa, FL: University of Tampa, 2009. Originally published in 1984.

Board, Prudy Taylor. *The Renaissance Vinoy: St. Petersburg's Crown Jewel*. Virginia Beach, VA: Donning Company, 1999.

Bousquet, Stephen C. "The Gangsters in Our Midst: Al Capone in South Florida, 1930–1947." *Florida Historical Quarterly* 76, no. 3 (Winter 1998).

Breslauer, Ken. *Historic Sites and Architecture of St. Petersburg, Florida*. Denver, CO: Outskirts Press, 2011.

Brown, Lynne. *Gulfport: A Definitive History*. Charleston, SC: The History Press, 2004.

Brown, Warren. *Florida's Aviation History: The First One Hundred Years*. 2nd ed. Largo, FL: Aero-Medical Consultants, 1994.

Capone, Deirdre Marie. *Uncle Al Capone: The Untold Story from Inside His Family*. Bonita Springs, FL: Recap Publishing Company, 2012.

Cool, Kim. *Ghost Stories of Clearwater and St. Petersburg*. Venice, FL: Historic Venice Press, 2004.

Cushman, Joseph D. *The Sound of Bells: The Episcopal Church in South Florida, 1892–1969*. Gainesville: University Press of Florida, 1976.

Davies, R.E.G. *Airlines of the United States Since 1914*. Washington, D.C.: Smithsonian Institution Press, 1972.

Davis, Enoch Douglas. *On the Bethel Trail*. St. Petersburg, FL: Valkyrie Press, 1979.

Davis, Jack E. *An Everglade Providence: Marjory Stoneman Douglas and the American Environmental Century*. Athens: University of Georgia Press, 2009.

Deese, A. Wynelle. *St. Petersburg, Florida: A Visual History*. Charleston, SC: The History Press, 2006.

Deitche, Scott. "Al Capone in St. Petersburg." *Informer Journal* (October 2012).

DeLorimier, Finnette Gilbart, and Charles T. deLorimier. *The Saga of Two Sojourners: The Memoirs of Finnette & Chuck deLorimier*. Newark, DE: Bullfrog Publishing, 2000.

De Quesada, A.M. *Baseball in Tampa Bay*. Charleston, SC: Arcadia Publishing, 2000.

Dunn, Hampton. *Yesterday's St. Petersburg*. Miami: E.A. Seeman Publishing, 1973.

Fountain, Charles. *Under the March Sun: The Story of Spring Training*. Oxford, UK: Oxford University Press, 2009.

Fuller, Walter P. *St. Petersburg and Its People*. St. Petersburg, FL: Great Outdoors Publishing Company, 1972.

Gould, Rita Slaght. *Pioneer St. Petersburg*. St. Petersburg, FL: Page Creations, 1987.

Grismer, Karl H. *The Story of St. Petersburg*. St. Petersburg, FL: P.K. Smith, 1948.

Hartzell, Scott Taylor. *Remembering St. Petersburg, Florida*. Vols. 1 and 2. Charleston, SC: The History Press, 2006.

———. *Voices of America: St. Petersburg*. Charleston, SC: Arcadia Publishing, 2002.

Homan, Lynn M., and Thomas Reilly. *Wings Over Florida*. Charleston, SC: Arcadia Publishing Company, 1999.

Hurley, Frank T., Jr. *Pass-a-Grille Vignettes: Times Past, Tales Remembered*. N.p.: privately published by Friends of the Gulf Beaches Historical Museum Inc., 1999.

———. *Surf, Sand, & Postcard Sunsets: A History of Pass-a-Grille and the Gulf Beaches*. N.p.: privately printed, 1989. Originally published in 1977.

Jackson, Page S. *St. Petersburg: An Informal History*. St. Petersburg, FL: Great Outdoors Publishing Company, 1962.

Lantrip, Gary. "Profile: Frederick E. Guest II." *Tampa Bay Life* (September 1990).

Ling, Sally J. *Al Capone's Miami: Paradise or Purgatory*. Deerfield Beach, FL: Flamingo Press, 2015.

Marth, Del. *St. Petersburg: Once Upon a Time*. St. Petersburg, FL: City of St. Petersburg, 1976[?].

McCarthy, Kevin M. *Aviation in Florida*. Sarasota, FL: Pineapple Press, 2003.

———. *Baseball in Florida*. Sarasota, FL: Pineapple Press, 1996.

Moffi, Larry, and Jonathan Kronstadt. *Babe Ruth in Florida*. Haverford, PA: Infinity Publishing Company, 2002.

———. *Crossing the Line: Black Major Leaguers, 1947–1959*. N.p., n.d.

Montville, Leigh. *The Big Bam: The Life and Times of Babe Ruth*. New York: Doubleday, n.d.

Mormino, Gary R. *Land of Sunshine, State of Dreams: A Social History of Modern Florida*. Gainesville: University Press of Florida, 2005.

———. "Tampa at Mid Century: 1950." *Sunland Tribune* 26 (2000). Journal of the Tampa Historical Society.

Parry, Albert. *Full Steam Ahead!: The Story of Peter Demens*. St. Petersburg, FL: Great Outdoors Publishing Company, 1987.

Pasley, Fred D. *Al Capone: The Biography of a Self-Made Man*. Garden City, NY: Garden City Publishing Company, 1930.

Peck, Rosalie, and Jon Wilson. *St. Petersburg's Historic African American Neighborhoods*. Charleston, SC: The History Press, 2006.

———. *St. Petersburg's Historic 22nd Street South*. Charleston, SC: The History Press, 2006.

Pederson, Paul. *Build It and They Will Come: The Arrival of the Tampa Bay Devil Rays*. Stuart: Florida Sports Press, 1997.

Pinellas County Department of Environmental Management. *The Weedon Island Story*. Pinellas County Government Publication, 2005. Originally published in 1992.

Pinellas County, Florida. *The Constitutional Officers of Pinellas County: A Brief History*. Pinellas County Government Publication, 2006.

Reilly, Thomas. *Jannus: An American Flyer*. Gainesville: University of Florida Press, 1997.

Resendez, Andres. *A Strange So Land: The Epic Journey of Cabeza de Vaca*. New York: Basic Books, 2007.

Reynolds, Kelly. *Henry Plant, Pioneer Empire Builder*. Cocoa: Florida Historical Society Press, 2003.

Roberts, Elda M. *The Stubborn Fisherman: A History of the Roberts Family*. Port Aransas, TX: Creighton Publishing, 1970.

Rooks, Sandra W. *St. Petersburg, Florida*. Charleston, SC: Arcadia Publishing, 2003.

Schoenberg, Robert J. *Mr. Capone*. New York: William Morrow and Company, 1992.

Smithsonian Institution. *Annual Report for the Year 1879*, 1880.

St. Petersburg Yacht Club. *Centennial—A Nautical Heritage: The St. Petersburg Yacht Club Story, 1909–2009*. 2nd ed. N.p.: privately published, 2009.

Starkey, Jay B. *Things I Remember*. Reprint, Brooksville, FL: Southwest Water Management District, 1980.

Stevens, Julia Ruth, and Bill Gilbert. *Babe Ruth: Remembering the Bambino in Stories, Photos and Memorabilia*. New York: Harry N. Abrams Inc., 2008.

Stevenson, R. Bruce. *Visions of Eden*. Columbus: Ohio State University Press, 1997.

Straub, William L. *History of Pinellas County, Florida: Narrative and Biographical*. St. Augustine, FL: Record Company, 1929.

Taylor, Prudy. *The Renaissance Vinoy: St. Petersburg's Crown Jewel*. Virginia Beach, VA: Donning Company, 1999.

Turner, Gregg M. *Railroads of Southwest Florida*. Charleston, SC: Arcadia Publishing, 1999.

Vesperi, Maria D. *City of Green Benches: Growing Old in a New Downtown*. Ithaca, NY: Cornell University Press, 1985.

Wallace, Martha Rudy, "History of Pinellas County Republican Party." Manuscript, undated.

Wells, Judy Lowe. *C. Perry Snell: His Place in St. Petersburg, Florida History*. N.p.: privately published, 2006.

White, Gay Blair. *The World's First Airline: The St. Petersburg–Tampa Airboat Line*. Edited by Warren J. Brown. 2nd ed. Largo, FL: Aero Medical Consultants, 1984.

Williams, Eugene L. *My Life Story*. N.p.: privately published, 2010.

Wilson, Jon. *The Golden Era in St. Petersburg: Postwar Prosperity in the Sunshine City*. Charleston, SC: The History Press, 2013.

Young, June Hurley. *The Don Ce-Sar Story*. St. Petersburg, FL: Partnership Press, 1990. Originally published in 1974.

———. *The Vinoy: Faded Glory Renewed*. St. Petersburg, FL: Partnership Press, 1999.

Zazier, Marion. *The Beneficent Blaze: The Story of Major Lew B. Brown*. New York: Pageant Press, 1960.

Index

A

B

C

D

R

S

About the Author

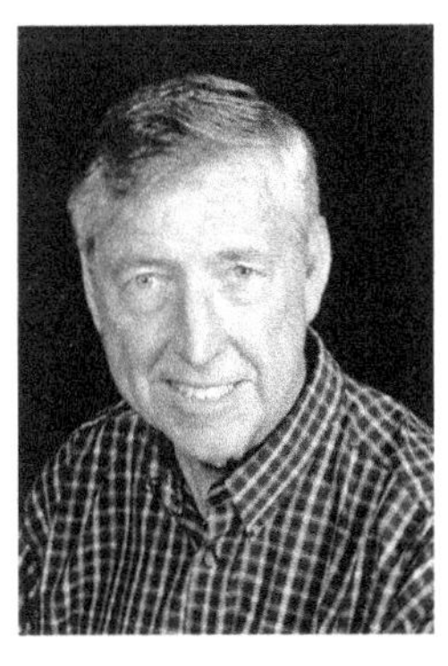

Will Michaels has served as executive director and trustee of the St. Petersburg Museum of History, vice-president of the Dr. Carter G. Woodson African American Museum, president of Saint Petersburg Preservation and president of the Flight 2014 Planning Board. Flight 2014 was organized to celebrate the centennial of the world's first airline, which originated in St. Petersburg in 1914. Community involvements have included service as president of the Council of Neighborhoods, design chair of the St. Petersburg Pier Advisory Task Force and member of the convening group of St. Petersburg Together. He is currently a commissioner on the City Community Planning and Preservation Commission. Will has a doctorate in anthropology from the University of South Florida and is a recipient of the Anthropology Department's Distinguished Alumni Award. He is retired from the United States Army Reserve as a lieutenant colonel. He has been a resident of St. Petersburg for more than forty years, is married to Kathy and has three adult children and four grandchildren. He previously authored *The Making of St. Petersburg.*

Other Works by the Author

The Making of St. Petersburg (2012), including:
The Making of St. Petersburg
The Spanish Invasion at Boca Ciega Bay
The Great Hurricanes
Civil War in St. Pete
Williams Park: Our Town Square
St. Petersburg's Piers: Anchors of the Downtown
The Fountain of Youth Rediscovered?
William L. Straub: Father of Our Waterfront Parks
Birth of Our County
World's First Airline
St. Petersburg's Passion: Baseball
History of Our Stadiums
Babe Ruth in St. Petersburg: A Soft Spot for Kids
St. Pete's First Entertainment Centers: Hard Acts to Follow
The Grand Hotels of St. Petersburg: Mainstays of the 1920s Boom
St. Petersburg: A Sense of Place

Published by the St. Petersburg *Northeast Journal*:
"The Snell-Bishop Home: A Marriage of Art and History" (2005)
"Celebrating the 4th of July in St. Petersburg" (2005)
"Our Oldest Neighborhoods" (2006)
"C. Perry Snell" (2006)
"John's Pass—Or Is It Juan's Pass?" (2006)
"Meddlers or Visionaries?: The Woman's Town Improvement Association" (2006)
"The Sunshine School: A State of Happiness" (2006)
"'Florida' Roberts—St. Pete's Most Famous Fisherman" (2007)
"Senator Henry Sayler: Friend of Presidents" (2007)
"The Challenge of Boca Ciega Bay" (2007)
"The Garden Cafeteria & Our Cafeteria Culture" (2007)
"Bill Cooper's 85 Years in St. Pete" (2008)
"Boyd Hill Nature Preserve" (2009)
"Dinning in Style: Ralph Graves, Jr." (2010)
"Title to the Pier Challenged" (2010)
"Landscaping the City: Phil Graham, Jr." (2010)
"Winter Home of the Amazing Mets" (2010)

“Personalities of the Roaring ’20s” (2011)
“Our Forgotten Mayor: Albert T. Blocker” (2011)
“Tony Jannus and the World’s First Airline Stamp” (2011)
“Our New Pier—A Sense of Place” (2010)
“Celebrating Old Northeast” (2012)
“World’s First Airline Centennial” (2013)
“Downtown Waterfront Master Plan” (2013)
“Equestrian St. Petersburg” (2013)
“Pinellas Point” (2013)
“St. Petersburg Country Club: Glorious Heritage” (2013)
“Marine Discovery Center at Our New Pier?” (2014)
“Bruce Watters Jewelers: A New Chapter” (2014)
“Bahama Shores: Florida Ranch-Style Architecture” (2014)
“Marine Discovery Features in New Pier Designs” (2015)
“Louie Hickman: Ninety Years of Sailing” (2015)
“New Life for the Tramor” (2016)
“Mayor Don Jones: Framework of Reason” (2016)

Other:

“St. Peter’s Cathedral History, 1889–1961”

Visit us at
www.historypress.net

....

This title is also available as an e-book

www.ingramcontent.com/pod-product-compliance
Lightning Source LLC
LaVergne TN
LVHW052337100826
845147LV00020B/1093

* 9 7 8 1 4 6 7 1 3 5 4 1 2 *